I0190827

DEAD RECK

A Review of Horror and the Weird in the Arts
Edited by Alex Houstoun and Michael J. Abolafia

No. 22 (Fall 2017)

DEAD RECKONINGS is published by Hippocampus Press, P.O. Box 641, New York, NY 10156 (www.hippocampuspress.com). Copyright © 2017 by Hippocampus Press. Cover art by Jason C. Eckhardt. Cover design by Barbara Briggs Silbert. Hippocampus Press logo by Anastasia Damianakos. Orders and subscriptions should be sent to Hippocampus Press. Contact Alex Houstoun at deadreckoningsjournal@gmail.com for assignments or before submitting a publication for review.

ISSN 1935-6110
ISBN 978-1-61498-212-8

Hallowed Readings for Halloween

Greg Gbur

ELLEN DATLOW and LISA MORTON, *Haunted Nights*. New York: Anchor Books, 2017. 368 pp. $16.95 tpb. ISBN: 978-1-101973-83-7.

As I write this, Halloween season is upon us again, with the leaves changing color, the nights getting colder, and the days getting shorter. It is a season that is filled with fun as well as foreboding, with princesses as well as poltergeists, with beauty as well as death.

Released on October 3, clearly to take advantage of the spirit of the time of year, comes the Halloween-themed anthology *Haunted Nights,* edited by Ellen Datlow and Lisa Morton. It contains sixteen original stories inspired by the Halloween holiday, as well as those more primitive celebrations that preceded it. The stories come from some of the most talented authors in short horror fiction working today, including Stephen Graham Jones, Jonathan Maberry, Garth Nix, and John Langan.

Haunted Nights continues a long and distinguished tradition of anthologies inspired by or set during Halloween—or at the very least intended to be read during a dark Halloween night. *13 Horrors of Halloween,* first published in 1983, was edited by Carol-Lynn Rössel Waugh, Martin Harry Greenberg, and Isaac Asimov, and contained a mixture of classic and more recent stories by luminaries such as Ray Bradbury, Edith Wharton, Ellery Queen, Al Sarrantonio, and Asimov himself. The 1986 anthology *Halloween Horrors,* edited by Alan Ryan, included stories by Ramsey Campbell, Robert Bloch, Robert R. McCammon, and Michael McDowell. More recently, Richard Chizmar and Robert Morrish's *October Dreams* (2000) featured work by Caitlín R. Kiernan, Poppy Z. Brite, Jack Ketchum, and others, and Paula Guran's *Halloween: Magic, Mystery, and the Macabre* (2013) has stories by Laird Barron and Steve Rasnic Tem and Melanie Tem.

This abbreviated list demonstrates both that there is a relatively constant demand for horror stories inspired by Halloween and that there are enough anthologies out there already that different takes on the concept would be welcome. Those who are familiar with collections edited or co-edited by Ellen Datlow will already know that she has a talent for collecting diverse and unique stories for a given theme, and the stories in *Haunted Nights* do not disappoint. There are stories that range from the suspenseful to the supernatural to science fiction to the surreal.

A short description of the stories will highlight this variety. The opener, "With Graveyard Weeds and Wolfsbane Seeds," by Seanan McGuire, tells a familiar story of teenagers visiting a haunted house on Halloween night—but this time, we see the tale from both sides of the supernatural encounter. Stephen Graham Jones's "Dirtmouth" tells a story of love and loss in which a grieving man visits the remote mountain wilderness where his wife died all too recently, and finds that there is betrayal in love even after death. In "A Small Taste of the Old Country," by Jonathan Maberry, two men who have fled their past to hide in Argentina find that their taste buds can give them away as much as their accents and mannerisms. The origin of one of Halloween's most visible traditions is explained in "Wick's End" by Joanna Parypinski, in a story that echoes classic legends of the devil's tricks.

A seemingly cruel treatment for a psychiatric patient opens Garth Nix's "The Seventeen-Year Itch," and shows how kindness can go horribly and unfathomably wrong. In "A Flicker of Light on Devil's Night," a struggling mother takes drastic steps to change her life in the season of the witch. Jeffrey Ford tells a ghastly story of body horror in "Witch Hazel," where it is explained how the quaint name of a local plant has its origins in deadly events of almost two centuries past. Tradition also plays a role in Kelley Armstrong's "Nos Galen Gaeaf," in which a young man attempts to manipulate his village's Halloween rituals in order to cause the demise of the girl he might love or hate.

In S. P. Miskowski's "We're Never Inviting Amber Again," the usual ploy to invite the sister-in-law to a party for some weird laughs and cheap spiritualism tricks backfires in a spectacular manner. Brian Evenson's "Sisters" starts out as a quaint story of young girls trying to enjoy the holiday, but metamorphoses into something much stranger—and its ending will shock. Elise Forier

Edie's "All Through the Night" looks at the tragic struggles of a woman in nineteenth-century New York City who has found that her infant has been replaced by an inhuman changeling. In Eric J. Guignard's "A Kingdom of Sugar Skulls and Marigolds," we explore the much different tradition of the Day of the Dead, and a sugar skull leads the protagonist on a journey of danger, violence, and hopefully redemption.

Paul Kane's "The Turn" captures that feeling of walking alone at night, feeling as if something is right behind you, needing to turn and look but not wanting to—and what awaits when you do. Pat Cadigan's "Jack" is a much more lighthearted tale of a supernatural trickster and those whose job it is to stop him from carrying out his wicked work. John Langan's "Lost in the Dark" is a detailed, lengthy, and unsettling exploration of a "found footage" horror film, and the real-life—and real-death—events that inspired it. The collection closes with John R. Little's "The First Lunar Halloween," a sentimental science fiction story about lunar residents trying to reclaim their heritage—and getting many more memories than they had planned for.

An excellent introduction by Lisa Morton provides a brief history of the Halloween tradition, its origins, and those celebrations that have paralleled it or arisen from it, which serves to provide context for some of the more curious settings of the collection.

In *Haunted Nights,* we have an excellent and diverse collection of tales by truly talented authors, set in the Halloween season. It is a perfect read for those who are looking to add some atmosphere to the holiday, or on any dark night before or after.

A Few Reflections

Martin Andersson

What struck me about NecronomiCon as early as 2015—and this is true about many cons—is that it is actually several separate cons gathered under the same umbrella. There is a film track, and a gaming track, and a very academic track, and a Lovecraft (and related topics, such as writers who influenced HPL or were influenced by him) track, and a modern weird fiction track, and perhaps others I'm not even aware of. It was quite possible to stick with one track and see the same people in the audience and on the panels, and to me, at least, that is a boon: there is a sense of continuity and intimacy that should be impossible at such a large con, and I can tune out all the white noise that would otherwise annoy me. Only once did I make a detour from my chosen track, and it was a complete waste of time—to me, that is.

The panels were of high quality, ranging from fair to truly excellent. Panelists generally did a very good job, with a few exceptions (I'll come right out and say that I'm a terrible moderator). Among the true highlights for me were the one on R. H. Barlow (even if I was on that one myself; I cannot, however, take credit for its success) and the one on the women of the Lovecraft Circle. Both topics have a great potential for book treatment.

I had promised myself to be more sociable this time and try to hang out with people, but the lure of interesting program items was too great. However, this can be viewed as a compliment to the con. Nevertheless, I still managed to talk to a few old friends and meet some new people I had previously known only from Facebook. And yet, I managed to miss some people who, it turned out, were there even though I never saw them.

Providence is a beautiful, beautiful city, and it would have been remiss of me to skip the tours. Just as in 2015, I took both the bus tour and the walking tour. It was a thrill to get reacquainted with the old sights and to see the plaque at Lovecraft's birthplace for the first time. And the grave always brings out deep emotions. Again, I was impressed by the knowledgeable tour guides.

Shopping is always a bane for me, and I have learned to travel light in order to accommodate the haul I always anticipate when going to cons. This time the haul numbered two dozen (!) books and journals, among which I would like to single out *Some Notes on a Nonentity* by Sam Gafford and Jason C. Eckhardt, *Dawnward Spire, Lonely Hill* by H. P. Lovecraft and Clark Ashton Smith, and a book from Smith's personal library. *Some Notes on a Nonentity* is one of the finest Lovecraft biographies I have ever read, and a must-have for any Lovecraftian.

If there was one cloud in the sky, it was S. T. Joshi's decision not to participate. The idea of a Lovecraftian con without Joshi's knowledge and insight is almost inconceivable to me (even though it obviously happened). I felt his absence very keenly on more than one panel that would have benefited *much* from his presence.

The Creature That Lives in the Dark

S. T. Joshi

RAMSEY CAMPBELL. *Born to the Dark*. Hornsea, UK: PS Publishing, 2017. 279 pp. £40.00 slipcased hc, £20.00 trade hc. ISBN: 978-1-786361-86-8.

This second volume of Ramsey Campbell's Lovecraftian trilogy of novels picks up on the threads of its predecessor, *The Searching Dead* (2016), and carries them considerably farther, setting up a spectacular dénouement in the final installment. Luckily, there is no need for readers to have read that first volume, as Campbell (through his first-person narrator, Dominic Sheldrake) summarizes its central incidents; but of course, a reading of *The Searching Dead* will add considerable nuance to Dom's pensive account of the frustrations he faces in getting those closest to him—both friends and family members—to believe the incredible tale he has to tell.

The story so far:

The Searching Dead, set in the Liverpool of the early 1950s, deals with the teenage Dom and his friends, Jim Bailey and Roberta (Bobby) Parkin, uniting as the Tremendous Three. But their friendship is severely tested when Dom secretly observes Jim and Bobby cuddling in a movie theatre—an act Dom takes as a kind of betrayal. That matter is cast into the shade when they all become disturbed at the actions of one of their teachers, Christian Noble, whose interest in the occult appears to have led him to gain the ability to raise the dead. In part through the actions of the three young friends, Noble's Trinity Church of the Spirit is set ablaze—but that in no way constitutes the cessation of Noble's various shenanigans.

As *Born to the Dark* opens, we have leapt forward thirty years, to the height of Thatcherite England in 1985. Bobby has become an investigative reporter, now partnered with a woman named Carole; Jim has become a policeman; and Dom himself is married to a woman named Lesley, with a five-year-old child, Toby. He teaches film at the university. Our concern through much of the novel focuses on little Toby, who has apparently been subject to seizures from infancy. In desperation, Lesley enrolls him in a facility called Safe To Sleep, which practices some kind of specialized sleep treatment. Initially, Toby seems to improve, but disturbing hints quickly emerge. Lesley tells Dom that Toby has "been scaring some of the children at school," stating that they may see "a giant face that lives in the dark" when they sleep. Toby himself describes some of his dreams about that face with unnerving naïveté: "It's like it's watching for you to go to sleep so it can have your dreams to make a bit more of itself."

Dom, who has been skeptical of Safe To Sleep from the start, wonders if Toby has managed to read the extracts of Christian Noble's diary—which contain all manner of cryptically cosmic passages—that Dom had copied in an exercise book. Dom also realizes that the name of one of the proprietors of the facility, a pediatrician named Chris Bloan, is a partial anagram for Chris Noble: could this be Christian Noble's daughter, whom he had referred to as Tina (i.e., Christina)? She herself has a son named Christopher (or Toph), an infant who seems incredibly precocious in numerous ways.

Dom's worst fears are confirmed when he sneaks onto the grounds of Safe To Sleep and sees the redoubtable Christian Noble himself come into the room where the children are sleeping. Noble, his daughter Tina, and her son Toph seem to be chanting the name Daoloth (a "god" created in Campbell's early *Inhabitant of the Lake* stories) over and over again. It is at this point that Dom experiences a clutching moment of terror when he attempts to flee the grounds:

> A wind that I couldn't sense was enlivening the foliage, which responded with a whisper unnecessarily reminiscent of the kind of hush you might address to a child who was unable to sleep. As the dangling carkins writhed they might almost have been striking to imitate the insects I saw everywhere I looked, squirming out of the trees but remaining embedded as if rather than nesting in the timber they might be extensions of the material. I was desperate not to touch them, especially those that reared up towards me, revealing how transparently gelatinous they were, as I tried

to sidle past the trees. When a bloated tendril found my cheek it felt like a cold dead tongue, somehow animated.

It gets worse. When, later, Dom goes to the hospital where Tina Noble works, he sees her making strange hand gestures over the newborn babies—and he comes to the staggering realization that she and her father have actually *induced* the seizures into Toby and other children so that her family can later gain control of them through their facility.

Horror and tragedy follow upon this revelation. When Dom frantically attempts to explain the situation to Lesley, she (perhaps rightly) believes that Dom is simply paranoid, a result of his boyhood encounter with Noble. She orders Dom from the house and immediately initiates divorce proceedings. (I confess that I found Lesley's sudden turning on her husband to be not entirely plausible. They had been married for at least six or seven years, but her extreme reaction—even if it was motivated by a desire to protect her son from what she believed to be Dom's harmful behavior toward him—does not seem wholly credible.) Dom comes to a dispiriting conclusion: "It looked as if I needed to protect Toby on my own, which left me feeling worse than isolated."

Things get worse for Dom before they get better. After confronting both Tina and Christian (both of whom appear to know who he is and what he has done in the past), Dom crashes his car near the facility after a hand-like object touches his face. He wakes up in the hospital with a serious head injury; his father, Desmond, is in the same place, suffering from the effects of an infection following a fall. And while Desmond is sympathetic to Dom's concerns about Toby and vows to take care of the matter, there is little Desmond can do; indeed, he dies shortly thereafter. At the funeral, Dom is disturbed when Toby makes the bland claim: "I don't think grandad's really gone." This may be nothing more than a conventional belief that Desmond is in heaven; but perhaps it has a more sinister signification?

Dom may not be quite as isolated as he thinks. Perhaps the Tremendous Three can take up the matter. Bobby becomes interested in investigating Safe To Sleep, and she wants Dom to fax her the extracts from Noble's diary; but Dom is dismayed (a word, incidentally, that Campbell tends to overuse) to find the diary missing. Can Toby, under Noble's instructions, have taken it? Bobby nonetheless carries on her investigation; but when she meets Dom later at a pub, he is startled to find that she has become a convert to Noble's ideas. "Tina Noble's doing everything she can for the children," she says, adding even more ominously: "I've joined in." She actually advises Dom to try a sleep session at the facility; Dom agrees—but he has other plans in mind.

During the session, Dom manages to wake up and clumsily take Toby away in his car. Noble, incredibly, seems fully aware of what Dom has done, but doesn't seem to care. In a brief confrontation he declares, "It matters much less than you imagine." Toby expresses a desire for his parents to be reunited, and Lesley drops her plans for the divorce. At a later stage Dom persuades Jim to conduct some private investigation of Safe To Sleep; but when they arrive there, they find the place almost entirely vacant. But that certainly does not seem to be the end of the matter; for in a dream Dom seems to hear Toph's voice saying: "You're ours when we want."

Born to the Dark is so powerful and skillful a novel that it is difficult to enumerate its virtues. For all that the first-person narration compels the reader to see events entirely through Dom's eyes, the portrayals of every other character—most notably the touchingly innocent Toby, but also the baleful and sinister Christian and Tina Noble—are razor-sharp. And if the novel is in one sense simply a bridge between *The Searching Dead* and the novel to follow, it is itself full of passages of both poignancy and terror that make it a gripping read in its own right. In particular, the cosmic reflections that come out of Toby's mouth, while fully in the language of an ordinary five-year-old, are extraordinarily potent:

> ". . . there's a creature that lives in the dark, only maybe the dark's what he is. Or maybe the dark is his mouth that's like a black hole or what black holes are trying to be. Maybe they're just thoughts he has, bits of the universe he's thinking about. And he's so big and hungry, if you even think about him too much he'll get hold of you with one of them and carry you off into the dark."

And that culminating scene, where Dom and Jim explore the deserted facility—especially its baffling cellar, where the floor appears to be twisting in a kind of vortex, like a shell—is a passage of quintessential horror fully equal to analogous passages in prior weird fiction, ranging from H. P. Lovecraft's *The Case of Charles Dexter Ward* to Caitlín R. Kiernan's *The Red Tree*. Campbell here is doing nothing more than expressing humanity's age-old fear of the dark—but he does so in a manner as plangent and chilling as anywhere in his entire corpus of writing.

There is more to *Born to the Dark* than merely moments of terror. Even if only incidentally, Campbell has sharp words about contemporary culture clashes on both the right and the left. He makes no bones about the fact that Desmond Sheldrake is a religious and racial bigot (indeed, a substantial portion of *The Searching Dead* was devoted to Dom's—and, one suspect's, Campbell's—slow renunciation of the Catholic faith in which he was raised). But Campbell is careful to suggest that Desmond's attitudes were common to the people of his generation. Campbell is also pungent in dealing with leftists—especially with a sort of curdled liberalism that takes quick offense at the most innocuous of remarks. Colleen Johns, the divorce lawyer Lesley has hired, becomes an infuriatingly smug figure, twisting Dom's words to what she fancies is her client's advantage. When Dom casually mentions his friend Bobby, the following colloquy occurs:

> "Is this something else I ought to know about, Lesley?" Colleen Johns said.
> "Good God, you're eager for material, aren't you?" I protested. "She's a lesbian."
> "Do you have some problem with that, Mr Sheldrake?"

First, Colleen is slyly suggesting that Dom is having an affair with Bobby, or at least is more than just friends with her; then, when Dom denies it, she does a bait-and-switch and hints that Dom is a homophobe! No wonder everyone hates lawyers. It later becomes evident that Colleen is simply using Lesley's case to advance her own anti-male agenda ("Every successful case is a blow struck for all of us" [i.e., all women purportedly under the thumb of patriarchy]). Campbell's own position seems to be a sort of middle-of-the-road sanity, eschewing the religious bigotry, racism, and sexism of prior generations but not going so far as to become a mindless captive of identity politics.

The one element where the novel may come up short is its

purportedly Lovecraftian substratum. The references to Daoloth are too slight and tangential to be fully comprehensible; presumably they will be cleared up in the next novel. What we are led to infer, insofar as we can make any sense of the supernatural manifestations involved, is the notion of astral projection—which is certainly not a Lovecraftian conception. (Campbell refers several times to Rose Tierney, the protagonist of his earlier novel *The Parasite* [1980], where astral projection is suggested.) The raising of the dead might be a nod to *The Case of Charles Dexter Ward*, but it is so common a motif in weird fiction that no specifically Lovecraftian implication need be assumed.

Born to the Dark ranks among Campbell's finest novels, and it will leave every reader in anticipation for what promises to be a chilling conclusion to the trilogy. It must be emphasized that the pleasure derived from this book—as from Campbell's work as a whole—extends far beyond its shuddery passages. The purity and elegance of his style; the deftness of his portrayal of character; the skill with which psychological and supernatural terror are interweaved—these and many other elements place Campbell at the pinnacle of contemporary weird writing, and perhaps all weird writing. His only feasible rival is himself.

Worthy Wordsmithery

Tony Fonseca

JASON V BROCK. *The Dark Sea Within: Tales & Poems.* New York: Hippocampus Press, 2017. 349 pp. $20.00 tpb. ISBN: 9781614981947.

One way to sum up Jason V Brock's new collection, *The Dark Sea Within,* would be to quote Brock himself, who in his preface states that the collection "is a work that I hope offers some modicum of insight into, or at least thoughtful examination of, our shared human condition." In that respect, the collection is an admirable one. Its stories explore greed, guilt, love, dependence, and hubris, and they offer not a pat but a complex exploration of these traits. In addition, Brock is a wordsmith, and this comes across with every line of poetry and prose, resulting in passages like this gem, from the poem "A Carcass, Waiting": "We are but a shadowed agent of tomorrow / And the mournful sentinels of yesterday, / So while the moment erodes from remembrance / We celebrate our decay."

Unfortunately, Brock has one blind spot in this collection, which is a lack of subversiveness. What I mean by that is that his stories end exactly where it seems they should end—which makes some (but not all) of them predictable, and it makes all of them less cynical. In other words, Brock opts for endings that do not necessarily explain what happened, but explain too clearly why it had to happen. In each story's premise is its ending. Horror, dark fantasy, and weird writers need to be subversive, especially in a genre that has been around for 150 years. In order to stay fresh, writers need to think about variant endings rather than the usual one where everyone who deserves to be punished (or unwittingly opens a box) is punished. In the poems, it leads to a tendency to explain meaning, rather than to let images wash over the reader. The quoted passage from "A Carcass, Waiting" would have been the perfect end to a poem about the human condition—but it is not. Unfortunately, the poem continues, and more unfortunately, explains itself to the reader.

This leaves the question of what is most important in a story or poem: does writing skill trump vision? With this collection, I am minded to answer that it does. Brock's writing style reminds me of Robert W. Chambers (whom I adore). He is clever when cleverness is a virtue; he is succinct when clarity is essential; and he is surreal when it is necessary to tip readers on their heads and create a sense of wonder. Like Chambers, Brock has an eye for detail and penchant for phrase turning, and in some ways, a similar degree of linguistic mysticism (the sense of the sentence presents itself in time). And he is engaging at all times. Love the stories and poems in Brock's collection or hate them, no reader can ever accuse Brock of writing boring prose or verse. These pieces invite reading, and that is 90 percent of the battle for a writer. As he explains in his preface, "building things takes sustained effort . . . one word, one brush stroke, one frame after the other . . . each bit becoming part of the mosaic of a (hopefully) worthwhile endeavor."

In this same preface, Brock explains that he writes "all kinds of things and feel[s] no urge to be defined by, or even embrace, a genre." He goes on to point out that, nonetheless, his worldview tends to be a dark one, one that results in stories that are a nice combination of "erotica, Magical Realism, fantasy, literary, and other forms of expression." This is certainly one strength of *The Dark Sea Within*. On the whole, it attempts to be (to quote Brock) "the literary equivalent of someone like David Bowie—[with the final goal being] to challenge others. . . . To be unafraid . . . [to be] meditative, outré, diverse, and often misunderstood." Or to put it another way, these stories are an example of what Brock calls Dark Magical Realism. Whether there is an inherent irony in trying to create (or redefine) a genre while striving to be "genre-less" is for readers to decide. I will take as Brock's intention that his writing is not one of the recognized fan genres of horror, science fiction, or the new weird. But *Dead Reckonings* is a review of horror, and coincidentally, these tales and poems work well as horror, sometimes psychological and sometimes cosmic; therefore it is in that light that I read them. As horror, they succeed—they are atmospheric, offer a sense of personal or societal dread, and invite a darker worldview. In addition, readers who are partial to dense prose, with lots of description and digressions, will enjoy this collection, as Brock's style embraces both.

The two best tales in the collection, "Transposition" and "The Shadow of Heaven," are good examples of this. "Transposition" is one of the tightest stories in the collection, with fewer digressions and what I would call unnecessary description (that is, descriptive passages that add no necessary information but are there for stylistic purposes). The tale of a modern-day team of grave robbers in the form of a surgeon and his twin brother, an addict ex-nurse who now works for a morgue, is an engaging one, although the ending was telegraphed much too early (when it is reported that the sleazy partner of the twins had found two transplant donors). I would have personally preferred a less expected ending—for example, a more cynical one where Aiden, the hubris-stricken surgeon, would have quietly continued the final face transplant even though the "donor" was his twin brother, for after all, it would have been a crowning achievement to his career and therefore very much in line with his character, even knowing that he would soon be the victim whose eyes would be harvested. "The Shadow of Heaven" is just one of those perfect stories—a tale of cosmic horror set in the Antarctic that leads inexorably where such a story should—with a monolithic creature (or creatures) rising from the depths to threaten all humanity. Such a creature is introduced in this wonderful passage:

> It started as a soft rolling on the water; then an object more than a mile across thrust up from the sea, perhaps a couple of hundred feet from the USS Higgins. The shape dwarfing the destroyer was vast; it seemed to sparkle from within as though some swallowed, ancient future galaxy shone through its ebon, sea-drenched skin. In another eternal instant, the great being—dripping with kelp and seawater, glimmering in the vivid dawn like some unearthly, newborn titan—reared up to its full, multi-storied height.

Such description is both the strength and weakness of this collection. When it works, as in the aforementioned passage, it is brilliant. When it does not, it comes across as an exercise in wordsmithery. For example, in the opening tale, "The Dark Sea Within," details of scenery or post-coital action are occasionally given, but when they do they have little import on the narrative, thus making them slightly distracting. What makes such description even more puzzling is the fact that in places where description is absolutely called for, it does not always happen. One excellent example from this story occurs when David, the tale's main character and a man whose greed has become his blinders, meets with an arts dealer claiming to have an undiscovered Bosch. The meeting is simply left to the reader's imagination, I suspect to avoid giving away the tale's ending (although Brock is a skilled writer and could have easily created an atmospheric and ominous scene without tipping his hand). Furthermore, in "The Dark Sea Within," including an important scene like the art purchase would not only have produced what could have been the best part of the story, but would have also provided further information about David, enough to better explain the nature of his demise, since magical realism works best when the reader has enough information to understand the relationship between the metaphor-as-metamorphosis and the narrative logic as established.

The same type of "scene skipping" occurs in "Windows, Mirrors, Doors," a nice, compact story about an elderly woman's final days. The tale takes the reader right up to the final scene, where her body is found after she begins seeing deceased relatives in her mirror, but rather than narrate the discovery through a consciousness (doing so through hers would have been brilliant), the text font changes and the narration turns into what appears to be a storyboard, explaining what will happen when she is found. While some readers may appreciate the narrative experimentation here, I personally felt cheated.

The same can be said of "The Man with the Horn," which contains an inexplicable juxtaposition of heavy-handedness (the name of the ominous noisy neighbor is Mr. Trinity—oddly enough, a fact that is somehow totally lost on all who encounter the mysterious old man) and surreal narrative. This left me thinking the same as with "The Dark Sea Within," which is: why this event, this character, this ending? Not enough is known about the narrator to explain why her fate is, well, fated. I was also left scratching my head when a poem suddenly appears out of nowhere and when the narrator tells a real estate agent, "We don't have any. I mean, no children. . . . I decided we weren't having any." The narrative notes that she felt strange saying it aloud, but the reader has to ask, why would she say it at all to a stranger?

All that said, again my final estimation is that the stories are well worth the attention of fans. I reiterate, Brock is a wordsmith. He knows how to construct a sentence so that readers get sucked in, whether it be because of a beautifully worded philosophical musing and play on words ("In her estimation, hearts only served a few purposes at this life stage—heart attacks, heartbreak, heartache") or to create a sense of dread and fear ("Building in intensity, the tenor of his instrument was mournful, the melody a wailing dirge—a cacophonous mélange of cawing, rasping, weeping shrills and squawks—which seeped through to her . . . filling her head, filling the night, filling the world with its anguished, doom-laden call").

All personal nitpicking aside, I recommend this collection to readers who are looking for new, exciting voices in the genre, whether those voices be horror, science fiction horror, dark fantasy, or dark magical realism. For starters, the tales themselves are clever and show that Brock's dark vision has a well-developed, consistent sense of itself. In addition, many of the tales have a thoughtful, meta-textual property. For example, "Windows, Mirrors, Doors" references a couple of stories from the collection, as well as a few quotations from T. S. Eliot that are used in other tales. "The Man with the Horn" references characters from the story that immediately precedes it, "The Dark Sea Within." Tales like "Memento Mori" offer clever twists on old tropes (in this case, that of the doppelgänger), and poems like "Fallen: A Lament and Affirmation" offer engaging images and use of phrasing, as in the lines (which describe Lucifer's descent), "Creating an arc of cold flame as / He flashed through the soundless void— / tumbling, / spiraling, / drifting, / spinning . . . / For an eternity of communion with / Dark matter, pulsars, and distant asteroids." Such wonderful metaphysical language is immediately juxtaposed against the physical: "Billions of years passed again as, / screaming His anguished song, / Lucifer careened through Space-Time at 186,282 miles/second." The text also includes not only the tales and poems, a few of which are original to this collection, but also artwork by Samuel Araya, Jason C. Eckhardt, and Brock himself. For those readers who like to know about influences and intentions, Brock also offers a lengthy, detailed, and personable Notes section at the end of the collection. And finally, the collection has a very nice treat for readers, the tale "Afterlife," co-authored with Sunni K Brock and the one-and-only William F. Nolan.

A Visitor to Arkham

Ramsey Campbell

My childhood was haunted by many things, among the most pleasant of which were glimpses and rumours of the weird in published form. From a very early age I got to know many of the classics of the field by borrowing anthologies on my mother's tickets from our local Liverpool public library (then housed in a narrow room in a block of small shops in Childwall). Among many other dark delights, I read several tales by Lovecraft—most overwhelmingly, "The Colour out of Space," which I found profoundly disturbing—and wished I could find more. That may have been my first experience of the allure of the apparently unobtainable. The original *Weird Tales* was another case, lodging in my mind for years after I saw an issue in the window of a general store in Southport. I yearned for the monstrous visions it appeared to promise, but at seven years old I wasn't allowed to buy such a lurid item

The prohibition was lifted once I turned ten, a marvellously opportune development, because Thorpe and Porter (publishers of quite a few British editions of American fantasy and science fiction magazines) were just remaindering their excess stock. At least one Liverpool tobacconist had cartons full of them, each stamped sixpence, and my pocket money went that way for months. I believe it was in one of the digest-sized issues of *Weird Tales* that I found an ad for Leslie Flood's postal book service, and soon I bought earlier issues from him. Some advertised forthcoming Arkham House books—forthcoming, that is, in what was already my past—and I assumed they were as out of my reach as the moon. This only made them more alluring, and the titles of some of the contents conjured up hints of wonders and terrors that needed no further words: the dweller in the gulf, the nameless offspring, the thing in the cellar . . . Their suggestiveness blossomed in my mind, and Arkham House felt like the haunted place in which they grew. I may even have derived a strange kind of contentment from the idea that I would only ever be able to fancy what the books contained, as if the material inhabited my imagination alone and gained power from its very lack of definition. I'd call that a sort of magic.

I was in my teens before the magic became physically real, when I saw my first Arkham House book. Leslie Johnson (a founder member of the British Interplanetary Society and of the Liverpool Science Fiction Group) was a science fiction bookseller who dealt from his house just a few minutes' walk from mine. I no longer recall how I learned about him, but I still remember the awe that overwhelmed me when I saw an Arkham House book on a shelf of his office. It was *Witch House,* which he'd ordered for a customer who appeared to have let him down. Leslie promised it to me if the customer didn't show up soon, and I imagine I may even have prayed that he wouldn't, though I was on the way to leaving religion behind. Whatever the reason, the book stayed unclaimed until it became mine.

While it's pretty untypical of Arkham and certainly lacks any Lovecraftian elements, I devoured it nonetheless, and obsessively reread the titles announced on the back cover, which gave me new images to feast upon: the lurker at the threshold, the space-eaters, the thing that walked on the wind ... Even then I thought the books containing them were long gone, and if I hadn't bought a run of several years of James Taurasi's *Science Fiction Times* I might have continued in my ignorance. Seated in my old front garden on a sunny day, I believe I let out a cry that might have been audible throughout the neighbourhood. Among the typed mimeographed paragraphs in a recent issue, and undistinguished from them until my eye lit upon it, was an announcement of books forthcoming from Arkham House.

I ordered every one of them through poor Leslie Johnson— poor, because then I pestered him with the thoughtless persistence of the worst kind of fan, ringing him from a phone box each day to learn if the books had arrived. Did I hear his wife call "It's him again" or some announcement of the kind, followed by a prolonged pause that might have denoted his trudge to the phone and, who knows, a grimace or a mouthed response before he told me yet again that no, they weren't there yet? Eventually they were, and perhaps his and his family's relief was as great as mine.

Even the little brochures announcing future Arkham books gave me real pleasure, and I read them again and again, not realising that some Arkhams weren't to be: *Worse Things Waiting* had to wait for Carcosa to bring it out, and *Away and Beyond* went away too. Over the years I came close to collecting a full set of Arkhams, missing just the first two Lovecrafts and the fabulously rare Leah Bodine Drake, until the demands of home ownership made me sell almost all the books in the early seventies. (I couldn't bear to part with the Hope Hodgson omnibus.) I did replace some with the Neville Spearman editions, but despite being offset from the originals they're hardly the same: they lack the magic (and in the case of *Skullface,* the pages are diminished too, taking the font with them). I also bought some later Arkham titles, but they're a token presence on my shelves. I'm no longer much of a collector, and my owning a complete Arkham set these days is as unlikely as a complete run of *Weird Tales*.

Now I must backtrack to the fulfilment of a dream I would never have dared to have. Without Arkham House I might never have been professionally published—specifically to begin with, without the massive assistance of the house's massive personality, August Derleth. At the beginning of the 1960s I wrote a handful of stories imitating Lovecraft as closely as I could. My friend Pat Kearney, the British fanzine editor and later historian of the Olympia Press, and the American fan Betty Kujawa suggested I should send them to Derleth for his opinion. I don't think I expected more than that—certainly not that he would offer to publish them if I applied the detailed editorial suggestions he provided. I was even luckier to get such editing at the start of my career than I was to be published. I'd imitated Lovecraft's occasional stylistic excesses without taking anything like his care with structure, verbal or narrative; I'd even set the tales in Massachusetts when I'd never been out of England. I rid myself of all that to my and the world's considerable benefit, and was rewarded when Derleth bought a tale for a new Arkham anthology (*Dark of Mind, Dark of Heart,* a title that dropped its prepositions prior to publication). Two years later, though he was (understandably) not entirely satisfied with it, he published my first book.

He bought my second book as well, though it was radically different from the first—so much so that I very nearly despaired of sending it to him at all. Sadly, he died before *Demons by Daylight* could see print, and I felt I'd lost far more than an editor— he had been more of a father figure than my actual father. S. T. Joshi has collected and edited all our surviving correspondence in *Letters from Arkham*. *Demons by Daylight* was eventually ushered into publication by the shadowy presence of Donald Wandrei. I never met him, and deduced only years later that he had written the blurb.

Alas, Wandrei was the cause of an incident that came close to damaging my relationship with Arkham House. He came to distrust Forrest J. Hartmann, then the lawyer for the publishers and for the Derleth estate, and as a result Wandrei took legal action against him and Arkham House. In July 1973 Hartmann wrote to me "I must report that Donald Wandrei has gone through a complete personality change and is no longer with Arkham House. Moreover, he has been doing some rather wierd [*sic*] things lately and should you ever receive any correspondence from him, I would appreciate being advised. This is particularly sad when you consider that Don is one of the top men in the field even though he is at retirement age . . ." I copied this to my agent Kirby McCauley, who sent a copy to Wandrei, his old friend. Wandrei made it public, which apparently could have been interpreted as evidence that I was working against Hartmann. An uncertain time followed, even once I'd written the lawyer an apologetic letter at Kirby's urging, but I met Hartmann when I visited Arkham House in 1975, and we made our peace. Dwayne Olson sets out an objective account of the Wandrei incident in his afterword to *Don't Dream,* and finds in Wandrei's favour, though acknowledging that the author descended into paranoia near the end. At some stage of this Wandrei wrote to me, describing me as a real writer but dismissing Derleth as a hack. Augie himself admitted that he wrote too much too fast, but he also produced plenty of fine work.

I did meet Wandrei's successor, the late James Turner, a volatile fellow. This was during that 1975 visit, when I spent several pleasant days walking Derleth's walks (though I took just a couple of steps onto his favourite railway trestle) and in general being made at home by the personnel of Arkham House. Jim had, shall we say, strong opinions, and perhaps felt the need to establish his editorial personality. Arkham had already commissioned me to edit *New Tales of the Cthulhu Mythos,* but during my stay we argued over my intention to include a new story by Karl Edward Wagner. Jim apparently felt Karl's "Sticks" had been lacking, and informed me bluntly that if I bought a tale from Karl the anthology would be killed. Later he must have changed his mind, for he anthologised "Sticks" himself.

I don't mean to denigrate Jim. He was at least as supportive as his predecessors. He encouraged my experiments in *The Height of the Scream* and later proposed a collection to represent my first three decades, *Alone with the Horrors.* It was a magnificent tribute by a great publisher, and (as it sadly proved to be) a fitting end to our association. In 1997 Jim was dismissed from his position, reportedly for letting science fiction dominate his list, and was replaced by Peter Ruber. Somewhere around the turn of the century, April Derleth asked me to put together a new collection for her to publish, and in time I did. This was Ruber's response.

Dear Ramsey,

Thanks for letting Arkham House consider your latest story collection, "Told By The Dead." I regret very much that it doesn't fit our schedule at this time.

Because we published 4 of your previous collections, I feel obliged to mention that I had problems trying to read most of the stories all the way through. While they contain fragments of excellent narrative prose, too often the stories come across as intellectual exercises—that is, they describe a mood or a reaction to something perceived as a horror but lack a focused plotline. With a few exceptions, they seldom reach a satisfactory conclusion one way or the other, and come across as being very murky, ambiguous and obscure.

Aside from that, there's been a significant shift in customer purchases over the last three years indicating a trend back to more traditional ghostly and fantasy storytelling; and not surprisingly, a growing demand for non-fiction, historical and biographical books about the pulp fiction era and its writers. As we have a limited publishing schedule, we have to actively pursue a mix of projects and, accordingly, reduce the number of our fiction titles.

We know there's a small niche market out there that likes the kind of stories you write and that you have a loyal following. A publisher catering to that horror market would probably be more successful in selling the book than we would.

I've packed up the manuscript portion of your collection and will air mail it to you this week.

I wish you every success in placing "Told By The Dead."

Best regards,
Peter Ruber, Editor
Arkham House Publishers, Inc.

I confess to being taken aback, since the stories were certainly no more obscure than some of the contents of *Demons by Daylight* and *The Height of the Scream,* both published by Arkham. I've never argued with a rejection, but since April had asked for the book in the first place I dropped her a line. She'd gained the impression that the tales were science fiction, and invited me to try Arkham House again if I returned to my typical mode. In fact just one short tale in the book is science fiction, and *Told by the Dead* found a home at PS Publishing, where it received the British Fantasy Award. That brought my Arkham publications to an end, except for a poor early tale included in *Arkham's Masters of Horror,* edited by Peter Ruber. I didn't read his prefatory essay about me until it saw print, but it was mostly accurate, despite an odd contention that I attended night school to obtain an equivalency diploma (news to me, unless my memory is more senile than I think).

PS Publishing is now my Arkham House, and by no means only mine. All the same, I'll always be hugely grateful to Arkham and to August Derleth in particular. Without them I may never have been heard of. I was more than happy to repay my debt, however meagrely, by writing the introduction to one of four volumes of Derleth's supernatural tales, published by the Battered Silicon Despatch Box and stocked by Arkham House. Not only was the book graced with a reprinted cover by Matt Fox, quite possibly the weirdest of the *Weird Tales* artists and for me inseparable from that magazine, but I had the pleasure of inventing a title of the kind Augie might have conceived: *The Sleepers and Other Wakeful Things*. May it help to keep his memory alive, and may Arkham House live on.

A Journey Beyond All Journeys

(*Condensed*)
Donald Sidney-Fryer

How did it happen that I, Donald Sidney-Fryer, attended the Lovecraft convention at Providence, Rhode Island, the Necronomicon III, 17–20 August 2017? Because the people behind the con make a point of having a poet laureate during the con's duration—in accordance with the civilized literary standards associated with fictioneer, poet, essayist, and epistolarian H. P. Lovecraft (1890–1937)—my chief publisher Derrick Hussey, the owner-editor of Hippocampus Press, proposed my name to the chairman, Niels(-Viggo) Hobbs, for the role or position of the current event. Niels accepted the proposal. Thus I became not just one of the guests of honor but according to the official literature a special guest of honor, thus a double recognition, as properly registered by myself, as honoree, and with gratitude.

After finishing up my more or less last project, or part of a project, the big, long-awaited leave-taking for the con took place. Traveling from Sacramento, California, on American Airlines or affiliates, we arrived in Providence an hour later than scheduled, 11 P.M. instead of 10 P.M., due to the lateness of the connecting flight out of Chicago. Otherwise it turned out a routine flight.

I hoisted up my bags once more and soon found myself at last in the Providence Biltmore, my temporary abode for five nights and four full days, Thursday, Friday, Saturday, and Sunday. Laying down my bags, I found myself alone at last, free from other people. I slept until I awoke before 8 A.M., dressed, and went down to eat my breakfast in the fine restaurant maintained in the hotel. Then I returned to the peace and quiet of my suite, to study my part in the convention's program. Niels had arranged a full schedule for me, but generally with enough space between events so I could take a break in the bar off the dining room, or rest in my private chambers.

Derrick had benevolently published what might remain my very last book, *Aesthetics Ho!: Essays on Art, Literature, and Theatre,* which concludes with what is indeed my last collection of poetry, *Ends and Odds,* thus balancing out my previous volume, the autobiography *Hobgoblin Apollo,* which concludes with my previous collection of poetry, *Odds and Ends*. At my request Derrick timed my latest book's appearance to coincide with the H.P.L. con in Providence. For this last volume I had created two tributes, one in prose, one in verse: "H. P. Lovecraft—A Belated Homage" and "To. H.P.L.—A Tribute out of Time," respectively.

The opening ceremony took place at the First Baptist Church, in the upper and grander of the two main auditoriums contained in this very large historic space, Barnaby Evans acting as emcee and opening the program. Steven J. Mariconda followed with a fine and finely delivered account of Lovecraft's life and career, and then a local woman, an excellent historian, recounted some of Rhode Island's historical firsts achieved as a colony and then as a state, mentioning the often close connections between these events and those in Lovecraft's fiction and poetry. However, this estimable lady demonstrated very few of these connections beyond simply mentioning them, that is, hardly at all, alas! On their own these revelations of Rhode Island's past as colony and state proved rather amazing.

Summoned to come forth at the very last, I presented three short but appropriate sonnets of my own, ending with the recently written "To Howard Phillips Lovecraft—A Tribute out of Time," which features pointed and suggestive references to his cosmic-astronomic-mindedness, to his fabled and fictitious tome, the *Necronomicon,* to several tales major and minor, as well as to his Ancient Ones. Like everyone else featured on the program, I used the handy microphone—a marvelous invention indeed. For me the highlight became the "perfect musical accompaniment" (per the program literature) as provided by the indeed internationally renowned organist Gigi Mitchell-Velsaco, a trained operatic soprano as well. In fact, until someone explained it to me, I had thought that two performers presided at the organ, the organist and the singer.

I had wanted to confer with Gigi, not only to talk with her about her superb performance but to discuss the modern and inherited repertoire of organ music, not just J. S. Bach and Max Reger but Franz Schmidt. *His* organ works remain large-scale symphonic morceaux of enduring fascination and supreme value, if not in fact the culmination of the First Vienna School, from Haydn and Mozart through Brahms, Bruckner, and Mahler, but all founded on the "magical" and abundant organ works of J. S. Bach. Gigi finished her "accompaniment" with a brief but very cute version of "Yes! We Have No Bananas," followed by the Prelude and Fugue in C Minor of J. S. Bach. This piece reminded me that his organ works after all remain music for performance in church or temple.

I shall give as compact an account as I can of the con per se, but mostly my part in it. Friday, Saturday, and Sunday went by so fast, as I ran from one place to the other, that in memory it seems no more than a fast-moving kaleidoscope. Zip goes the film!

On Friday, 18 August, I served on a panel discussing that singular author Ambrose Bierce, who influenced so positively George Sterling and Clark Ashton Smith. In the early afternoon I appeared on a panel discussing the latter poet and fictioneer, a highly gratifying experience. Finally during the late afternoon all nine or ten guests of honor made their appearance and introduction on a panel, superlatively moderated by s. j. bagley. He ran in front of the table with the panelists from one to the other, an amazing demonstration of intellectual, emotional, and psychic power. Friday terminated with the Eldritch Ball (masquerade) from mid-evening to midnight or so. I did not attend but went to bed early instead.

Saturday for me went by no less rapidly. I appeared on a panel anent Arthur Machen in the early afternoon. Thanks to Lovecraft and his great admiration for Machen (shared by Ashton Smith), the Welsh author occupies today an universally respected and acknowledged position in the weird fiction genre. Then came two panels on weird poetry, the first in the late afternoon, ably and sensitively augmented by Frank Coffman, the professor and specialist on the copious poetry of Robert E. Howard. The real revelation here was the brilliant classical Greek scholar Sonya Taaffe as the adroit moderator, when at my humble request she recited the opening lines of the *Odyssey* in classical Greek. What an apocalypse!

The final poetry panel, scheduled as a workshop, proved even more apocalyptic than the first, thanks to the younger poets who held forth, or as in the case of Stanley Gemmell, an established and authoritative poet of unusual strength but apparently without a published collection. He should have served as the elder poet present, not myself. Stanley read with an unbelievable intensity a kind of love poem, celebrating some actual or ideal female beauty of the human species. Stanley projects poetry in the manner in which it should be: dynamic, clear, clean, with nuance and subtle humor; the ideal of serious play that constitutes poetry on the highest level. His recitation or reading utterly knocked me down, knocked me over—unprecedented and overwhelming!

On Sunday morning I woke up too late to attend the "Cthulhu Prayer Breakfast," that is, without entering conspicuously late, anathema to me. Nobody had scheduled anything for me on Sunday, a panel or what-have-you (for which I give thanks). Although I had wanted to attend a panel on William Hope Hodgson in the early afternoon, I stayed instead in my room, attended to personal needs, and exercised, subsequently taking a nap. Once awake, I dressed and circulated, and joined a late-afternoon group in the hotel bar with Derrick and others for drinks and food. Thus the day completed itself.

Apart from Gigi's excellent organ performance on Thursday, one other thing happened that meant as much to me, perhaps even more. Getting to know, becoming acquainted with the remarkable poet Stanley Gemmell (and no less personable an individual) became on Saturday afternoon the con's highlight for me. He had brought with him a whole pile of my own books (authored or edited) for me to sign for him, always a highly flattering ritual for any author, particularly one as esoteric as myself. We were sitting outside the capacious room where the Arthur Machen panel discussion would occur.

During our exchange various other aficionados came up to me and also had me sign copies of my books, some of them recently purchased in one of the vendor rooms. Even the pleasant young man on duty as a "minion" outside the door to the Machen panel went and bought a copy of *The Atlantis Fragments* (in its trade paperback edition) for me to sign! All this proved quite gratifying, to say the least. I have so few genuine admirers of my literary arts that I cherish any and all of them as long-lost family, if not children, given my age of eighty-three.

On Sunday evening, after parting from Derrick and company, I returned to my room, but not before I had a long and significant exchange with the individual named Christopher Geissler, the director of special collections at the John Hay Library at Brown University. Librarians in general remain my favorite people, if not culture heroes; very well informed and often impassioned, but in an understated manner. Christopher proved no exception, and we discussed the manifold riches of the Lovecraft Collection, which also includes abundant papers, letters, and manuscripts of stories by Ashton Smith, as safeguarded and then donated by Lovecraft's nephew R. H. Barlow. Cosmic blessings on Bob Barlow for preserving such and so much precious documents!

During the latter morning of Monday, 21 August 2017, by pre-arrangement, my cousin Gail's husband Paul had driven over from their home in East Sandwich, in northwest Cape Cod, and came to pick me up while at the Providence Biltmore. At that point the most rewarding and extended part of my sojourn began. I had arranged my flight back to Sacramento so that I could spend special time with Gail and Paul, and also with Ron, Fran, and Glenn (brother, sister-in-law, and their eldest son) not quite 50 miles northwest of Portland, Maine. I had not visited any close relatives in the Northeast for quite a few years, and NecronomiCon III provided the perfect means, benedictions on Derrick H. and Niels Hobbs.

Curating Ars Necronomica 2017

Brian L. Mullen III

Curating an art show is something that always fills me with awe. The skills that all the artists use to achieve their visions is, as an artist myself, something I always marvel at. Techniques that are foreign to me and approaches to subject matter that I never considered taking are one of the great joys of curating a group show. Wonder is universal in the lineups that we have had for all our shows, but it is this very wonder that singles out this year's guest of honor out from the crowd. Getting to work with John Jude Palencar was something that amazed me with how fortunate we are with the Ars Necronomica shows. To work with an artist of that caliber and level of skill gives one pause, as does getting to hold one of his paintings in my hands while hanging the show. To have a level of intimacy with works of art that are so perfectly orchestrated and show a skill so refined and precise makes all the efforts worthwhile.

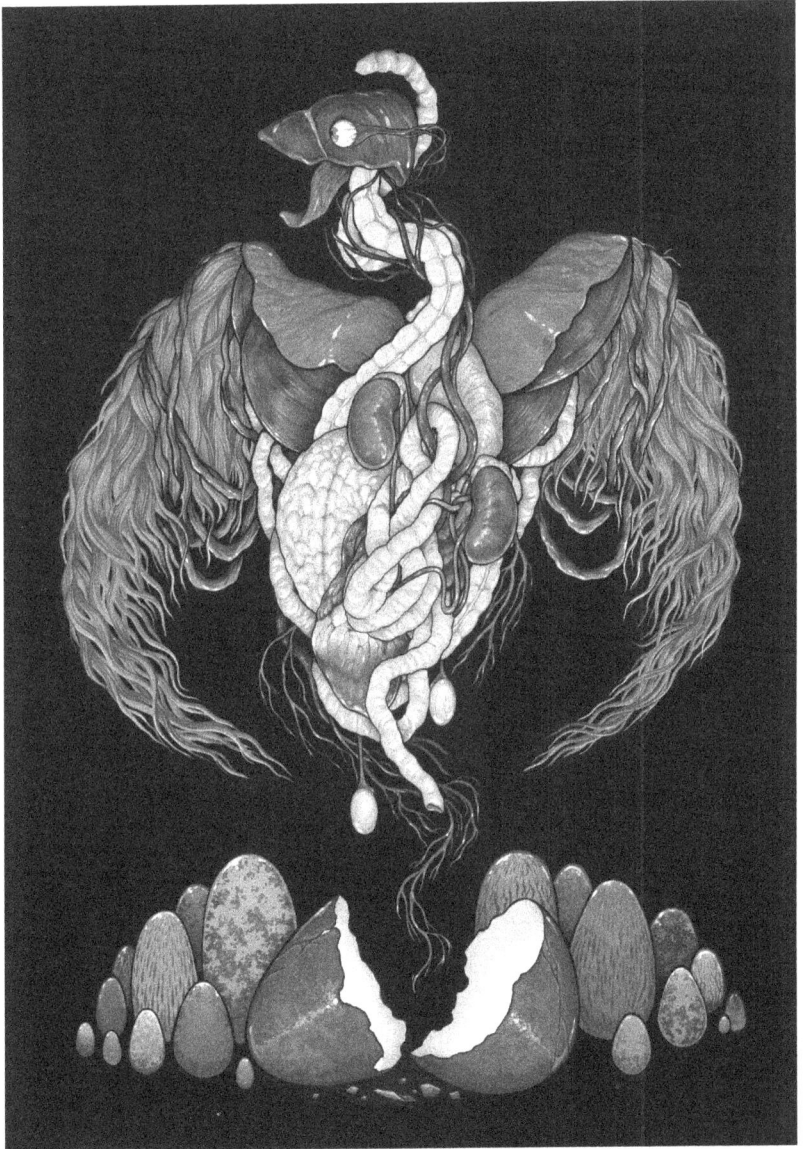

Jeanne D'Angelo, "An Egg a Month"

This year's was by far the most successful show we've had on many levels, and much of that is owed to the amazing locale and the exemplary staff at Rhode Island School of Design's Woods-Gerry Gallery. Mark Moscone and his team made hanging the show easier than it had ever been and, I think, displayed a level of skill in laying the show out that exceeded anything we could have done without them. The normal process where we work with the gallery was minimal, as the eye they have and the knowledge that they used—which spaces would work for what pieces—was beyond what any outsider could have brought.

Also, for the first time this space felt natural for us, which I personally think is important to the overall success of a show. The architecture of the building seemed to bring a life to the work that sterile white walls could not do on their own. Take, for example, how perfectly Michael Knives's 20+-foot-long sculpture hung in an alcove, against a backdrop of woods that Lovecraft would have been able to see from the windows of his final earthly residence. Or how perfectly Lee Joyner's sculpture of H.P.L. and his inner demons showed in the foyer on a single pedestal placed in the middle of the space. Perhaps it was something about how the light would come through the old windows of this amazing old New England–style building that provided the perfect way to admire work. Every year Woods-Gerry had been in the minds of the organizers of NecronomiCon, and after this year I truly believe we have found a home most perfectly suited for the future of the Ars Necronomica.

The feedback we received from the artists who were in attendance has been incredibly positive. The previous years' shows, although always considered a success in content and execution, seem in retrospect to build up to the perfect union of space and content of this year's exhibition. And for the first time we were able to show all the art in a single location, whereas the previous shows were in two or three galleries. And although the separate shows still had a fantastic composition (if I dare say so myself), getting to put all the artists under one roof solidifies and unifies the lineup and makes the show greater than the sum of its parts. I believe I speak for everyone on the board of curators when I say that we will have our work cut out for us to try and improve upon this year's show. Hopefully we are up to the task.

Dead Reckonings

The Wonders of the Visible Weird: Ars Necronomica 2017 and Guest of Honor John Jude Palencar

Dave Felton

17 August 2017. It is a warm evening to walk up College Hill in Providence, Rhode Island, shortly after the opening ceremony of NecronomiCon-Providence. Even with brief stops on the way to note historical points of interest, the New England humidity clings to clothing and skin. Attendees arriving at RISD's Woods-Gerry Gallery are flushed with both heat and anticipation, for the convention's art exhibition, Ars Necronomica, has opened. Featuring 100+ works from seventy-three artists, visions of cosmic horror and dread are conjured in paint, graphite, and ink, sculpted in clay, cast in bronze, suspended from wires and caught under glass . . . an almost overwhelming menagerie of the weird inspired by the fiction of H. P. Lovecraft. But it's not all tentacles and shoggoths: this year's show, along with the convention's programming, has stretched feelers out to embrace a larger and more diverse body of work, evidenced by illustrations that depict scenes from Clark Ashton Smith, William Hope Hodgson, Edgar Allan Poe, and Margaret St. Clair, among others. With such a collection on display, it is obvious that this year's Ars Necronomica is larger in scope and ambition than previous incarnations in 2013 and 2015, and for most Lovecraftians who have come out this evening the highlight of this year's show is the convention's artist guest of honor, John Jude Palencar.

He has illustrated J. R. R. Tolkien, Ursula K. Le Guin, and Stephen King, but it was his wraparound covers for Lovecraft collections published by Del Rey that captured our wicked imagination: *The Dream Cycle of H. P. Lovecraft: Dreams of Terror and Death* (1995), *The Transition of H. P. Lovecraft: The Road to Madness* (1996), and *Tales of the Cthulhu Mythos: H. P. Lovecraft and Others* (1998). These paintings became synonymous with Lovecraft's Mythos for a generation of readers, and to the joyous excitement of all present these works hang in this year's show.

The canvases are unexpectedly large, each over three feet wide; viewed from a distance, the nightmarish horizon of "Dreamcycle," with its darkened buildings and columns of smoke, stretches behind stone stairways that ascend to nowhere and stage-like platforms for demons and skeletons to prance upon. Another lifeless landscape lies behind the central figures of *The Road to Madness,* where impossible mountains and ancient ruins serve as backdrop for an insane performance of twisted and tortured actors. In each painting the deliberate arrangement of geometrical shapes constructs the illusion of framed space, making it a place of performance and surreal theater. Step closer to these paintings and the viewer is rewarded with the rich detail of Palencar's technique—a multitude of tiny paint strokes, linear and contoured hatchings of color that form the appearance of realistic surfaces, layers of brushwork that capture the translucence of skin over flesh. The hands he creates on canvas are expressive enough to appear real—tendons and veins stretch across metacarpals, dirt rings fingernails, palms open and fingers clutch. With his anatomical accuracy and realistic style, Palencar could easily paint recognizable facial features, but instead he often fashions mask-like aspects for human figures with skulls that look more like disguises than actual human skulls, as if they are worn for a role to be played. These stylized masks fit perfectly in the theatrical space Palencar has created on canvas, but what is the play and what roles do the twisted, screaming, leering figures enact?

The deranged anatomy—subject to brush-laid boils, impalement, amputation—is body horror at its finest, but in Lovecraft the horror of the body is its betrayal and the revelation of its secrets. Questionable lineage manifests itself as physical abnormalities and weakened, unreliable mental states in his stories, and we see these ideas reflected in Palencar's *Tales of the Cthulhu Mythos.* One figure screams in horror as his lower torso morphs into scale-like shapes, another is entirely silenced by a mouthless alien head transplanted onto its human host, becoming in the process bizarrely mutated with displaced intelligence. As paperback covers, readers already initiated in the Mythos might recognize themes from "The Shadow over Innsmouth" and "The Whisperer in Darkness," and longtime fans of the Lovecraft circle and weird art might point out Palencar's homage to Lee Brown Coye—

floating sticks above a desolate lunarscape—but to new readers who might come across these covers in a store or online, the beautifully surreal figures and shapes demand, at least, inquiry and investigation. How many have bought their first Lovecraft book based on these images by Palencar? They must be legion.

Palencar poses for photos next to his paintings as some fans wait nearby for a chance to speak with him and get a closer look at his paintings, though it's obvious that many at the opening reception don't recognize him and seem to be seeing his work as if for the first time. This is impossible given Palencar's broad portfolio, which includes covers for books that have appeared on the *New York Times* bestseller lists. Perhaps because his art has been formatted for publication—title, author, and publisher text added to and painted over his images, which themselves are often chopped and shrunk for their destined format—and because this art has become part of objects associated more with the author and title than the artist himself, Palencar has existed for decades in a strange limbo, where even if you liked his work you might never have looked to see who was responsible for it. His three large paintings done for the Del Rey Lovecraft collections are so detailed and loaded with symbolic imagery that they look like densely interwoven puzzles; now displayed in this year's Ars Necronomica show and experienced at the size conceived by the artist, they exist as new things for Lovecraftians to discover, with illusions that simulate a sense of vertigo, as if the viewer might fall into portals that frame Palencar's surreal world if one were to stand too close. It was a gift to have these covers shown at the Woods-Gerry Gallery that weekend, as it is the first time these three paintings have been shown together—an event that will remain in the minds of everyone present.

There is so much art in Ars Necronomica 2017, too much to take in during the two-hour opening reception when many of the artists included in the exhibit are in attendance, some of whom have made long journeys to be here in Providence, like Denmark's John Kenn Mortensen, Germany's Fufu Frauenwahl, and Italy's Sara Bardi. Over the next several days a good number of the artists will be found in NecronomiCon's vending rooms, offering prints, magazines, sculptures, shirts, and original art that can be found nowhere else. Robert Knox, for example, brings a table full of painted canvases and miniature sculpts to every convention, and this year plans to sell original cover art for *Crypt of Cthulhu*. Sam Gafford and Jason C. Eckhardt have brought copies of *Some Notes on a Nonentity*, their graphic novel on Lovecraft's life recently released by PS Publishing, and they are scheduled to discuss the work and sign books at a Saturday morning panel. Gage Prentiss, who is tasked with sculpting a life-sized bronze figure of H.P.L. that will eventually be erected at the bottom of College Hill, has brought silicone shoggoths with eyes that glow in the dark. Liv Rainey-Smith, a woodcut printmaker from Portland, Oregon, will share a panel discussion with Palencar himself during the convention and has brought affordable prints of her work that draw upon historical and traditional esoteric art. And the convention's artist guest of honor will be found on several of the weekend's panels, after which he will likely be signing and inscribing copies of his book *Origins: The Art of John Jude Palencar*, published by Underwood Books.

The lights dim and the gallery begins to empty as attendees head toward downtown Providence, where weird festivities have already begun. There will be time this weekend to return to the gallery for longer views of the art, and on the way out artists make plans to meet and discuss all they have seen this evening. "John Jude Palencar's work was one of the first and most formative visual interpretations of Lovecraft that I ever encountered," artist Clayton Cameron reflects. "His paintings embody the grotesque sense of space that characterizes Lovecraft's writing, and seen in person, they reveal a consummate skill and startling subtlety that has deeply expanded my own regard for that work." Across the street from the gallery, at 65 Prospect Street, is Lovecraft's final home, where he wrote his last story, "The Haunter of the Dark," in 1935. Never could he have imagined that some eight decades later, the city would welcome fans of his stories to conventions and film festivals in his honor as his beloved Providence finally embraces him as its own. One of the co-curators of this year's Ars Necronomica, The joey Zone, takes much satisfaction in the evening and its close proximity to Lovecraft's house. "John's wraparound painting on trade paperback collections of Lovecraft set the mood for the offerings within, and his presence really upped the profile of our art show, hopefully establishing it as a player in successful exhibits of the phantastique, commercially and aesthetically. This collective vibrant weird not only makes Lovecraft look good, but all of us as well."

An Artist's Dreamworld Incantation: The Work of John Jude Palencar

Michelle Y. Souliere

John Jude Palencar. Say it three times, like a spell, and will he appear? No, but it sounds like a singular incantation, conjuring up seven magically stark panels for the Ars Necronomica exhibit of 2017, *Wonders of the Visible Weird*. In my case, it also happily results in a phone call from Ohio some weeks after NecronomiCon, just as the New England fall weather is beginning to set in. On answering my phone, I hear the words, "Hi, this is John Jude Palencar." So maybe it does work!

When I put Palencar's name forth as a nominee for the artist guest of honor for NecronomiCon 2017, little did I know that it was merely the tip of the iceberg. For years Palencar's elegant but somehow primal imagery for the Del Rey editions of H. P. Lovecraft collections, at least half a dozen so far, has haunted me. It wasn't until after the show, when reading through his art book *Origins,* that I realized how many Palencar book covers I had admired and sometimes loved over the decades. (Dozens and dozens!) Many have won awards, and to this day he quietly continues to accumulate honors and accolades in the illustration and fine art fields, both in the U.S. and abroad. But ask any random person if they have heard of this "John Jude Palencar," and chances are you will be greeted with a shake of the head and the reply, "No, who is he?"

This is how Palencar works. Silently, in the dark of night, insinuating his vision of a solid but elusive dreamworld in amongst the books we read. As he said himself when I interviewed him on the phone, "I have always been a night worker." While we sleep, he has been painting all our other worlds, silently, diligently, enumerating his visions one by one.

"After a while you get into this night groove, and it's kind of nice, you're master of your own universe. It's quiet, and you can control the environment through music or watching movies or whatever . . ."

In the stillness of the evening, there is less interference to work against, more room for the mind to move the paintbrush and find the way to transform disparate elements into something that ensorcels even Palencar himself.

"I have multiple easels in my studio so that I can have something set up on the other easel. It's real hard for me sometimes, because while I'm working on one, sometimes I'll start to fall in love with the other one and want to work on it [instead]. I'll glance around the panel [that I'm working on] and look at the other one, and say 'You know, that one area needs a little bit of work . . .' I'll be drawn like a moth to a flame."

Maybe that moth-to-flame focus is one reason his artwork tends to appear spot-lit—figures crouching, gesturing, almost-but-not-quite telling something important to the reader, or are they distracting us from the real lay of the land? Something is hidden in the shadows, over there, in the corner, and who knows what lies off the edge of the frame? Perhaps it is best not to know. Best to stick to the well-lit areas. But do we, the readers, play it safe? No. We pick up the book. We turn the page. We need to know—but we need to find the answers ourselves. As Palencar says, "I would rather create the covers that have more questions than answers. [. . .] People hate to be *told* things." His imagery is created to be a magnet for curious eyes.

Most of his problems with authors and art directors have come from attempts at over-management of his work. "If you do that, you're kind of killing what you probably hired the person [for], or what attracted you to the artist in the first place." A certain amount of direction is helpful, "but they really have to trust the artist," Palencar believes. In a worst-case scenario, this involves a situation such as he faced early in his career at home in Ohio, in a studio where "a lot of times they took your head away from you and just used your hands." Looking back on those years, he sees in them "the ugly underbelly of commercial art." It taught him that any time art direction takes a turn toward a "dictatorial" environment instead of a "collaborative" relationship, "the work suffers." The magic is lost, even if the job is completed successfully.

His next stage of work in the early 1980s, including his stint creating illustrations for *The Enchanted World* series published by Time-Life Books, gave him an appreciation for a different kind of art direction. *The Enchanted World* fed the imaginations of all those who read them, fueling their fancies with a feast of both modern work created specifically for the books and traditional artists' work that echoed each volume's themes. He estimates his work appeared in about ten of the volumes, and some of it is quite powerful. Those who own a copy of the *Ghosts* volume may recall the mysterious background paintings used at the beginning of the book, which were John Jude's. Those skull-like images lurking like masks in the shadows were revisited and amplified years later, as they reappeared in various guises throughout his artwork for the H. P. Lovecraft volumes published by Del Rey.

Asked about this recurring theme in his work, Palencar puzzled over it briefly, acknowledging, "I always liked the mask kind of thing . . . I don't know where that came from. It might be something to do with puppetry, and things like that, because I had marionettes when I was a kid, and in some cases I made my own marionettes along with the commercial ones that I had. I used to do shows in my garage—stuff aside from haunted houses, talk shows, all kinds of stuff." The habit of creating things of all types was instilled early on in Palencar's life, which he compared to growing up like the Little Rascals. "We would invent and build things, make our own fun. We used our creativity and were always encouraged. In that way my mom would always make sure we had white paper rather than coloring books, and stuff like that."

In the years since those early days of garage puppeteering, Palencar has continued to move forward, widening his grasp on the field of available spectators with every step. The growth of audience is part of his focus when illustrating book covers: one of his goals is to bring new readers to authors, a theme he returned to over and over again during our interview. The presence of that reach and that focus of intent in his work unites to make his imagery incredibly strong. Perhaps it is in part the cause of the paradoxical effect that makes his work so very visible, yet himself so *in*visible.

He sets the stage, carefully strews it with choice treasures to attract us into that peculiar Palencar landscape, leading us further in, only to step away out of sight once he sees we are enmeshed, feet set forward following the trail on which the words inside the book will take us. It is all ink and paint, all illusion, but once we make the choice to start reading, every bit of it becomes real, a journey initiated by the unseen hand of John Jude.

Truly there are other elements to his behind-the-scenes presence that are invisible when his paintings are used as book covers, and this was stunningly evident upon seeing some of his pieces in person for the first time at Ars Necronomica this summer. As he admits himself, during the exhibit "some people were saying they hadn't realized how large they were. Also the richness of the color and the texture. You don't see that when they're so small. Even though they're trade paperbacks, they still wind up being very small," when compared to the original size of the paintings.

The best chance fans have of seeing these pieces at something close to their true glory is in the mammoth Centipede Press publication, *A Lovecraft Retrospective* (2008), edited by Jerad Walters—a nominee for a special World Fantasy Award in the professional category for 2009. The volume contains the full-color wealth of decades of artists inspired by Lovecraft's work. With genuine admiration, Palencar recommends I find a copy if I am able to. "Those books are something to behold. I think the gatefolds are almost the size of the original [paintings]."

While his work ranges far afield, sometimes appearing in editorials, other times with fantasy or general-fiction books, he says in the end, "Horror is by far my favorite. It's a shame, because it's not really that popular in the overall scheme—fantasy is probably king, I would imagine, in all the genres so far as sales." That love for horror began at a young age, when his family would try to keep him from watching the horror movies shown some nights on local television. He was reasonably successful with his horror-watching endeavors, causing a fracas when his presence was found out . . . but only when it was too late!

"I snuck into the room when they said 'Don't let him come down—don't let John come down!' and they make a big deal out of it, so *of course* I'm going to want to [come downstairs even] more! And I'm like four or five years old trying to come into the living room and I saw the whole scene and they're like 'Oh my GOD, he saw the whole thing!!!' and 'He's going to be psychologically damaged!' and I guess I am because I became an artist." He laughs. "But I've always liked that stuff."

"The first horror story I ever read was 'The Dunwich Horror.' I got the book because I was interested in the guy's name. [. . .] I was like twelve years old or something, it was the Summer of Love [. . .] and the Sixties were going on, and 'This guy's name is LOVECRAFT, this is going to be a *hot novel!*' I started reading it and I go, 'This is not anything *like* what I thought it was going to be!' And then I really started getting into it, 'this is a *really cool* story!' Later on I was in junior high, and there was a TV series created by Rod Serling called *Night Gallery*. [. . .] They had an artist doing these cool paintings that I always liked, and I always looked at the technique. [I remember] not only being inspired by the art for that, but also noticing the stories that they were doing—'Hey, there's that Lovecraft guy again.'"

When I asked him about what parts of Lovecraft's fiction inspired him, instead of talking about his past work, he instead began looking forward. "I'd like to explore some of his creatures. I mean, I've seen everybody try to do these interpretations of Cthulhu and the Old Ones, I'd just like to try my hand at them and bring something different to them. I don't know what that would be. There are a couple of creatures, too, that he's done, and they sound really foolish—I think they probably look like some bad creature from *Doctor Who* or something. But I still think they could be brought to a more menacing, enigmatic [form]. I don't even know if I'd do the same kind of technique again—maybe I'd get a little bit more diaphanous, a little looser."

As we talk, he speculates on whether shifting away from the strictures of his usual egg tempera technique to another medium would allow for a more ethereal approach. "I know when I did Innsmouth I tried to incorporate some deep-sea fish with the creatures. It can get a little pulpy—B-movie scream queen kind of monster vibes going on in some of these things. I still think there's [another] way. [. . .] I can see something being done [by combining monsters] with all the other-dimensional [elements], and apparitions."

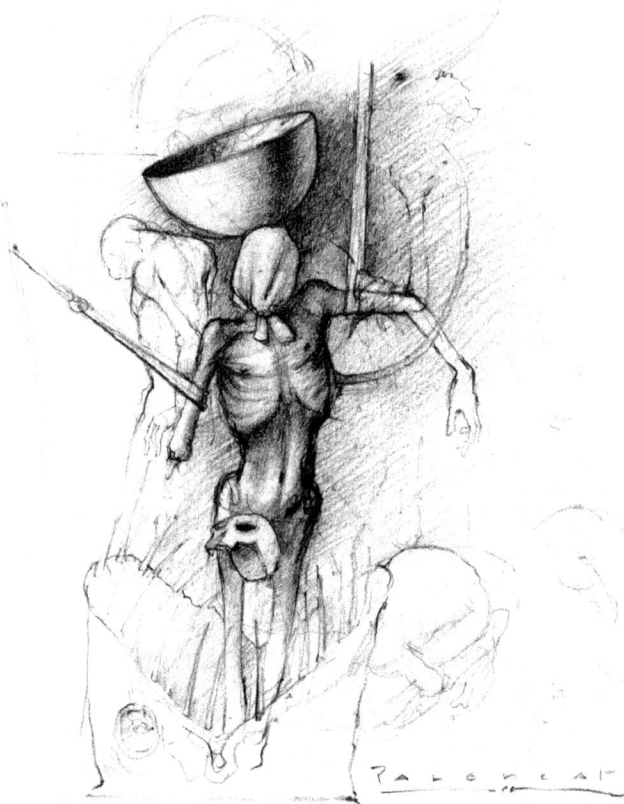

While his work tends to focus on the human forms that appear in his pieces, using them as a signal to the viewer, an entry point into the story of the piece, monsters and their forms have been a subject of personal interest since he was a kid. As he grew up he moved from making marionettes and homemade costumes to experimenting with practical effects used in monster movies. "I had a small book when I was a kid, I remember I was probably only eight or nine. It showed the special effects from movies like *Creature of the Black Lagoon:* they showed how they built the whole costume on the guy, and how he would be fed air so he could swim around and make it look like he could breathe under water. I was always fascinated by the 'how-to' stuff."

Early success came with some backhanded compliments, such as his brother winning first prize for Best Store-Bought Costume when in fact he was wearing a *Planet of the Apes* mask that Palencar handmade from latex and sheep's wool himself, gluing its multiple parts to his brother's face so he could make facial expressions and even drink coffee while wearing it. It appears that even early on, Palencar's creative illusions were so effective that his audience lost sight of him when under the power of their glamour!

All this simply reinforces my dawning realization that Palencar is a consummate artist: what he creates is as indescribable as Lovecraft's horrors. It is by turns enchanting and disturbing, but it is always exquisite, a coruscation of light and shade. The tension created by each of his images pulls viewers into a space that is different from any place they have encountered before. It is a space to absorb visually, it is a place that absorbs you into the story at the same time, without giving the ending away. It is the quiet of night that seeps through into your mind as you peer into the space, lit by the prospect of dawn or sunset—which? It matters not, only know that you cannot have shadow without light.

And as you open the roots that lie far back in your mind, exploring yet another of his images through the widening conduit of your eyes, a creature of unknown past and unseen present, whisper along with me, as you become part of the spell:

John Jude Palencar

John Jude Palencar

John Jude Palencar!

FOREVER and a Day

Jason V Brock

DARRELL SCHWEITZER. *The Threshold of Forever: Essays and Reviews.* Rockville, MD: Wildside Press, 2017. 218 pp. $14.95 tpb. ISBN: 978-1-479425-64-8.

> We all know the familiar cant. I've expounded it myself on numerous occasions: that Fantasy is the oldest of all forms of literature, the trunk of the primeval story-tree from which all else, including such Johnny-come-latelies as 'mainstream' . . . and even science fiction are but branches. There can be a touch of holier-than-thou when fantasy writers go on like that, the subtext being that *my* genre is older and deeper and more noble an undertaking than yours.
>   But there may be reasons to reconsider . . . .
>   —Darrell Schweitzer, "Reading the World's Oldest Novel:
>   Some Further Thoughts about Genre"

Darrell Schweitzer's newest nonfiction book, *The Threshold of Forever,* is a smorgasbord of reviews and writings from the insightful former co-editor of *Weird Tales*. The thirty-two pieces assembled in this collection range from 1999 to 2015 and find Schweitzer covering a wide swath of ground from old-school sci-fi ("Embracing Yesterday's Tomorrows, or Why We Still Read 'Obsolete' Science Fiction," "Why Stanley G. Weinbaum Still Matters"), contemporary creators ("Hooray Bradbury," "*On SF* by Thomas M. Disch"), horror fiction ("*Weird Tales* Past: December 1936," "Texts, Authors, and the Enduring Mystery of Edgar Allan Poe"), Lovecraft and his circle ("The Lighter Side of Death: Robert Bloch as a Humorist," "The Complete Poetry and Translations of Clark Ashton Smith"), esoterica ("People: It's What's for Dinner (All About Sawney Bean)," "William Beckford, Caliph of Fonthill Abbey"), and other interesting tangents ("Discovering James Hogg," "*Peter Schlemihl* and Other Classics That Nobody Reads"). The breadth of Schweitzer's interests is at once telling and impressive, whether he is waxing philosophical about ancient literature, discussing the impact of pulps on popular culture, or contemplating the concrete sociopolitical ripples of those who dared to imagine the future.

Some of the entries are very compelling, standing above the others with respect to scholarship and perception. Of these, I was particularly taken with Schweitzer's handling of the topics relating to Lovecraft and his reach in literature. Another stellar grouping involves Schweitzer's grasp of history generally, and science fiction literature specifically: he excels at bringing the strands of historical context and literary aspiration together in a way that not only piques interest in the subjects he is discussing or analyzing, but does so in an entertaining, relatable manner.

As with any work of this nature, there were a few articles that didn't particularly connect with me, but Schweitzer's engaging, readable style and good-natured sense of humor kept the book rolling. That noted, the volume is full of fascinating pieces, and the misses were few and far between. On the whole, this is an informative addition to any casual (or even learned) reader of fantasy, horror, or science fiction. Recommended.

The History of the Horror Fiction Boom in the 1970s and '80s

Stephanie Graves

GRADY HENDRIX. *Paperbacks from Hell: The Twisted History of '70s and '80s Horror Fiction*. Philadelphia: Quirk, 2017. 256 pp. $24.99 tpb. Illustrated. ISBN 978-1594749810.

Luridly contorted bodies, ghastly demons and devils, animated skeletons, buckets of dripping, oozing, and splattered blood, and sadomasochistic Nazi leprechauns—these are the images pop-culture journalist Grady Hendrix celebrates and taxonimizes in his new book, *Paperbacks from Hell: The Twisted History of '70s and '80s Horror Fiction*. Hendrix, an acclaimed horror author himself—his innovative *Horrorstör* (2014) and his self-aware teensploitation parody *My Best Friend's Exorcism* (2016) were both praised by critics—turns here to nonfiction, cataloguing the deluge of drugstore paperback horror novels throughout the 1970s and '80s in the

United States. Clearly a labor of love (and possibly obsession), in this survey he waxes rhapsodic about the cover illustrations that accompanied this genre, as well as nostalgically recalling the many now-forgotten authors and often outlandish and ludicrous plots that populated the horror landscape in this period.

Hendrix introduces the genesis of this work and his interest in the genre as stemming from his encounter with a copy of John Christopher's *The Little People* (1966), featuring the aforementioned sadomasochistic Nazi leprechauns terrorizing guests at a bed-and-breakfast housed in an Irish castle. The Hector Garrido cover—featuring the crenellation and spires of the castle with an army of the bullwhip-wielding Gestapochauns spilling forth from it—and the sheer insanity and outrageousness of the story itself led to his addiction to this particular subgenre of horror that proliferated throughout the '70s and '80s. Calling *Paperbacks from Hell* the "road map to his horror Narnia," Hendrix contextualizes the rise of this particular generic incarnation as a reaction to shifting social mores that embraced the "swinging '70s" ethos of sexual frankness and forwardness, as well as a capitalization on the success of landmark horror novels such as Ira Levin's *Rosemary's Baby* (1967), Thomas Tryon's *The Other* (1971), and William Peter Blatty's *The Exorcist* (1971), and on the successful film adaptations of the first and third. What follows is an exegesis on the pulp horror novels of this period and a detailed history of the publishers, authors, and illustrators behind them. Broken up by theme—Satan, creepy children, science gone awry, serial killers, etc.—Hendrix includes hundreds of cover art illustrations that detail a genre obsessed with anything creepy, outlandish, sexualized, or, preferably, all three; he points time and again to the "insanity vortex" that is often at work in these novels, as authors relentlessly exploited tropes and clichés to crank out work that was gorier, grosser, and more sensational in an attempt to snag readers in a glutted genre.

But Hendrix also exhibits a real love for the texts he details as well as a cultural awareness of these works as artifacts of their time, which were often directly reacting—as horror tends to do— to the world at large. For example, when covering the subgenre of haunted real estate or possessed lands, he offers historical context through his discussion of the 1970s "white flight" from cities and urban areas to suburban and rural areas. More importantly, he not only focuses on authors whose names and works have been lost to time, but also points toward writers working in this genre who were both successful and critically acclaimed. Later novels by Ira Levin as well as works by R. L. Stein, Christopher Pike, and Poppy Z. Brite are all mentioned, and Hendrix tracks the shift from pulpy redux of *Rosemary's Baby* and *The Exorcist* to the inescapable generic influence of works by Stephen King and Anne Rice evident in the early 1980s. He also considers the impact of shifting business models in the field, contrasting the proliferation of small imprints in the 1970s to their acquisition in the 1980s by larger publishers. Throughout the book, Hendrix also details the pen names and ghostwriting that is fairly commonplace in this field, especially focusing on the sixty-eight novels published under the name V. C. Andrews that were ghostwritten after her death by pulp horror author Andrew Neiderman.

Hendrix's knowledge of the genre is encyclopedic, and he deftly teases out connections between social shifts (such as the growing capabilities of technology or awareness of the 1980s AIDS epidemic) and the kind of novels that were finding their way to the marketplace, revealing cultural anxieties about computers, bodily fluids, immigrants, or heavy metal music. But as the shifting modes of publishing production eliminated the midlist phenomenon that made the pulpy horror genre possible in the first place, large publishers moved instead toward championing only novels they thought could be blockbusters. Hendrix bemoans this move away from the outlandish creativity that infused this period in horror fiction, but is grateful for the secondhand bookstores that still carry these novels and their wild interpretations of horror.

Although academics might be frustrated by the volume's lack of bibliography or references, there is an appendix that offers biographies of both the creators and publishers of this time period, and throughout the book Hendrix offers details about many of the cover illustrations and artists responsible for them. Overall, it's a terrific compendium of information on and collection of the cover art for the paperback horror novels that flooded the marketplace throughout the '70s and '80s, and a great resource for anyone interested in the forces of production at work in horror publishing during this time period.

Musings: NecronomiCon 2017

Alex Smith

I set out from the Omni with Jonathan Raab around lunchtime. The sun gave off the kind of heat you feel less on your skin than behind your eyes and under your lungs. Near the drained-looking Providence River, we passed empty construction lots enclosed by chain-link fences protecting unmanned excavators. I was mighty familiar with the constant grind of urban upsizing, and I wondered if this was what Providence was now.

When I was fifteen, I bought a beat-up Jove paperback of *The Colour out of Space* for a dollar-fifty. I didn't have the money to pick up one of the new, slick, matte-black editions coming out around that time, nor the courage to steal one. They were thicker, anyway. More intimidating. It would be three more years before I stuffed the unread volume into a backpack for some long train ride thinking, "Who knows? Maybe it's good." I'd likely only known of Lovecraft unconsciously prior to those little decisions that led me to reading a story about a farmer's family and a "blasted heath." Twenty years later Lovecraft had become a crucial part of my life, and the world of horror at large. *And* the lives of the 1500 like-minded souls who'd traveled to Providence solely to talk, think, and experience what Lovecraft had wrought.

Jonathan and I passed the Fleur-de-Lys Building with its framed scalloped yellow buds and cracked bay windows. I stopped to wheeze and take in the scene near the First Baptist Church. Narrow, tree-lined streets with tightly packed townhouses and humble lawns stretched into the distance. Each street formed part of the neighborhood covenant—its profound history lovingly preserved. Swiping a roll of sweat off of my head, I reminded Raab of the stories of Lovecraft's exhaustive walking tours of the neighborhood. When Lovecraft closed his eyes to die, he might have seen a place that looked something like this.

Having reached our destination atop College Hill, I admired a bronze bust of Lovecraft at the Ars Necronomica exhibit while I dabbed at my neck with a paper towel. In the bust, Lovecraft's face appears to be a mask strapped tightly to his head. Gnarly tentacles sneak from under the mask, hinting at something frightening hidden beneath the façade. I smiled at the monstrous Lovecraft bust, looked him in the eyes, fashioned a scant, imaginary exchange. I wondered what artwork surrounding him would impress him, amuse him, disgust or offend him. I knew that the camaraderie—the same kind he created when dragging his friends and admirers down the streets of Providence—still breathed and flourished on that hot day in August. I imagined he'd very like that very much. I reveled in that feeling—a sense that what underlay much of this convention wasn't weird media at all, but kinship.

On Monday I'm back in Maryland. Giant drops of rain fall for four minutes after lunch, creating saucers of black on the slate roofs of the suburbs. The humidity is stifling. Dizzied, exhausted, sort of sick, I heave myself into my truck and drive to my office in Washington. I love my work, but I'm keenly aware of a sense of loss. I want to be back there. I will try scribbling it away—think of what it felt like to be with my kin in Providence, think of that Lovecraft bust, the tentacled secrets hidden behind the mask.

In the Wild Beast Wood: The Triad of Mystery in the Artwork of Sidney H. Sime

Daniel Pietersen

"Any magazine-cover hack can splash paint around wildly and call it a nightmare or a Witches' Sabbath or a portrait of the devil, but only a great painter can make such a thing really scare or ring true. That's because only a real artist knows the actual anatomy of the terrible or the physiology of fear—the exact sort of lines and proportions that connect up with latent instincts or hereditary memories of fright, and the proper colour contrasts and lighting effects to stir the dormant sense of strangeness. I don't have to tell you why a Fuseli really brings a shiver while a cheap ghost-story frontispiece merely makes us laugh. There's something those fellows catch—beyond life—that they're able to make us catch for a second. Doré had it. Sime has it."—H. P. Lovecraft, "Pickman's Model"

In a similar vein to R. Murray Gilchrist, the now mostly forgotten author of weird fiction I talked about in the previous issue of

Dead Reckonings. Sidney H. Sime came from the north of England, ascended to giddy heights of recognition for his art—he was held in high regard by a certain strain of society, alongside the likes of Aubrey Beardsley and Harry Clarke—and then faded into the long night of obscurity. In Sime's case this is perhaps more through intent than accident—the collector Desmond Coke speaks of Sime's "contempt for fame"—yet is no less a shame for all that.

Born in 1865, in the Manchester borough of Hulme, a scant few miles across the Peak District from Gilchrist's Sheffield, Sidney Herbert Sime's early life was one of poverty and hard labor in the local area's Empire-fueling coal mines. Here the young Sime, employed as a miner, no doubt heard tales from the older hands of the mysterious and impish creatures that inhabited the mines: the bluecaps and knockers, cousins of the Germanic kobold, who often played small mischiefs on the miners but could also offer assistance to those in desperate need. It is not surprising, then, that the adult Sime, an imposing yet good-humored figure described quite wonderfully by Frank Harris as being in possession of a "tyrannic forehead," would profess an "inherent bent for the mysterious" and funnel that obsession into artworks that whirl the viewer off into strange lands, populated by even stranger beings.

As with my discussion of Gilchrist, this piece is not intended to be biographical but focuses on a handful of specific works that bring Sime's constant pursuit of mystery into sharp focus and tease out some of the horror theory that is held within. Those readers who would like to learn more about Sime's life are directed to the excellent *Sidney Sime: Master of the Mysterious* by Heneage and Ford.

Sime's work is wide-ranging in both subject and style; traditional figurative work blends into satirical caricature into fantastical vistas of varying levels of stylisation. You are as likely to encounter a cloud-wreathed giant as you are the caricatured features of some unfortunate pub regular. In this piece I will be focusing on three works taken from Sime's portfolio of fantastic and surreal imagery. This necessarily does Sime's myriad ability a disservice, for which I apologize.

Hish, an illustration taken from Lord Dunsany's *Gods of Pegāna* (1905), is one of Sime's masterworks. In depicting the eponymous "Lord of Silence, whose children are the bats," Sime for once eschews his tendency toward the baroque in favor of a simple structure: the figure of Hish, muffled in clinging robes, emerging from the eerily austere forest to go about his work and "maketh all noises still."

Hish's wood is dark, monochrome, and apparently devoid of life, but we know that bats, themselves mysterious and fleeting beings with a fell reputation, dwell within. The trees, as already mentioned, are obviously organic but strangely formed: uniform trunks, unnervingly straight, are topped with pipe-like branches and stippled sprays of foliage that look more like venting steam than leaves. All is still, frozen into silence by the passage of the Lord of Silence.

Hish is a liminal figure in both the illustration and the tales of Pegāna, perpetually suspended between the cavortings of the Lord of Dusk—who sends his shadow-children to "run about the room and dance upon the walls" as the other gods slumber—and the truly nocturnal fancies of the dream-god Yoharneth-Lahai or the fearful moon-howling of Wohoon, the Lord of Noises in the Night. Even in the creature's own portrait the layout of the illustration is sparse, with Hish having almost crept off the canvas and the vast majority of space left over to the strangely minimalist trees—an alien depiction of the natural world that would reappear in Eyvind Earle's hyper-stylised foliage or even the darker works of Roger Dean—or the tufts of coarsely sprouting grass. The depiction of Hish himself offers little in the way of explicit character beyond his strangely staring eyes and raised eyebrows; a bizarrely horrified expression for one who, by the end of his night's work, will have "slain all sounds." Rather, we can infer an intent from posture, a serpentine bend to the spine as one leg slinks forward, and the manner in which Hish clutches his swaddling robes close about his body. This is not a bold character like the haloed Slid, Lord of the Gliding Waters, nor even the corpse-god Mung, who is well known by god and man and, despite being lord of death, is considered to be the one who "calmed all who suffer."

Why is it then that Hish, a relatively minor and reclusive being in Dunsany's cosmology, should receive such a portrait? Sime uses the precarious position that Hish inhabits to make him an avatar of mystery. The piece becomes an exemplar of Sime's stated desire to enhance his artistic leaning toward mystery. Hish is a "hidden thing" going about "secret work," two potential translations of the Latin *mysterium* and the Greek *mysterion*. Yet the root of both these words is *myein,* "to shut up (the mouth)," from which we get the word "mute." Hish is not only a causer of silence but is itself silence incarnate, and it is in the hollows of silence that mystery lies like the deepest of fogs.

The forest reappears, still with the uniformly straight tree-trunks and shocks of foliage, in *Wild Beast Wood*. This time, rather than the conspiratorial closeness of *Hish,* the viewer is set beyond the tree line, looking back at the wood from a distance. A shadowy pack of feline creatures, their narrowed eyes glowing, emerges from the dense wood into a patch of moonlight that streaks down from a storm-wracked sky. The creatures head away from the trees, down a slight incline, toward the edge of the picture. Even held in the static capture of a painting, it is obvious that they move with a powerful grace and malevolent intent. Pinpricks of light between the trees promise yet more of the beasts. With this picture Sime once again presents the viewer with a mystery. What are these creatures? Where are they headed and why?

Wild Beast Wood is an invocation of the fear of the archetypal Dark, Dark Wood that pervades much of mankind's history. Whilst woodland, at least in the daytime, can provide shelter and sustenance, its nocturnal countenance is much more sinister. The fear that something antagonistic to our human way of life will creep out from the forest's edge, slinking and sneering, to raid our villages and steal away our children is very deep, very old. Yet what is the source of this fear? Is it that dark forests and the things that dwell within them are inherently inimical to humanity, or is it, perhaps more believably, our unconscious acceptance that by "civilizing" the plains we made the forest a haven for atavism and superstition? The straight trunks and shadow branches protect and hide older inhabitants of the earth, create for them a refuge.

The Hebrew word for refuge is *mistor* and its plural is *mistorim:* "the secret, mysterious places." It is the knowledge that something is happening to which you are not privy, in some removed place that you cannot access. The knowledge that something unknown is happening quickly turns to the fear that

Dead Reckonings

something terrible is happening, to the paranoia that something terrible is always happening. The creatures of the Wild Beast Wood could easily be literal monsters or figurative exhalations of fear, mysterious heralds of a greater terror yet to come.

Hish, then, is the mystery of silence, the pregnant dread of the about-to-happen, whereas the *Wild Beast Wood* is the mystery of emerging, the horror of the is-happening. The triumvirate is completed by the mystery of ending, the trauma of the has-happened.

In *When We Had Hunted the Moon Enough We Came Back Through the Wood,* an illustration from Lord Dunsany's *My Talks with Dean Spanley* (1936), we find ourselves back in the wood, trees now all around. Their half-domed crowns shed autumnal leaves down through the shafts of light that stream obliquely to the flower-strewn ground. Illuminated by one of these beams, bounding along a narrow path that winds between the tall trunks, are two creatures. They are similar to those who stalked out of Wild Beast Wood, still markedly feline but smaller. Possibly they are juveniles. Through the painting's title, these creatures now speak directly to us; the silence of Hish has passed, the implied dominion of humanity has ended, and now the spirits of the wood can talk freely. Yet their words are obscure and symbolic, laden with mystery. They have left the wood; they must have in order to "come back," after having "hunted the moon." What does this mean? We do not know, cannot know.

These three points in time—the about-to-happen, the is-happening, and the has-happened—show us mystery, a mystery that so easily turns to horror, from three different viewpoints.

The about-to-happen is the most obvious: a crisis point where actuality is still yet to bloom from possibility. The mystery stems from not knowing. Shirley Jackson's *The Haunting of Hill House,* a house that "watches every move you make," is a master class in the tension of the about-to-happen. There is a finale, obviously, but it is the inevitable dénouement of the truly tragic. The true story lies in the getting-there, walking through endless corridors as time flows by too thickly. For me, this part of the triad is akin to the horror of death. It is not death itself that is horrifying, because death necessarily negates the horror of death, but it is the slow, inevitable procession toward death that fills us with horror.

The is-happening initially seems to be anathema to mystery. If not knowing is mysterious, then how can knowing be mysterious? The answer is in how Sime chooses to represent the Wild Beast Wood—at a remove. When a point of view is fixed or otherwise constrained, then mystery fills the spaces unseen. In Hitchcock's *Rear Window,* for example, we are in no doubt that *something* is happening but because of the limited viewpoint we are forced into, we are not sure what it is and our imagination, like James Stewart's, begins to devour itself. For Sime, as for Hitchcock, the horror of the is-happening is not in the revelation but in the glimpse: the half-seen figure at a grimy window, the hand reaching out of the shadows. This is what I have come to describe as Exile: being removed from a position of agency to one of mere spectator, and a poorly informed spectator at that.

Moving from the is-happening to the has-happened is less of a stretch, as something that is happening will eventually, inevitably, move to having happened. Yet how can an ending be mysterious? By divorcing itself from its beginning. In *Stalker,* Andrei Tarkovsky's adaptation of the Strugatskiy Brothers' *Roadside Picnic,* some enigmatic event, one that perhaps has disjointed the causality of is-happening to has-happened, has created a place of corrupted reality called The Zone. In The Zone nothing is as it should be; neither physics nor spirituality follow the easy paths. The cause, occurring at some point in a time removed from our time, is no longer evident, and now there only lingers the inexplicable residue of effect. Effect without cause, having been dislocated from the flow of normal causality, is surely the shattering of sense into Madness. Is it coincidence that Sime here invokes the Luna and her obsessive cultists, the lunatics?

As Lovecraft notes in this essay's opening quotation, Sime uses "the exact sort of lines and proportions that connect up with latent instincts or hereditary memories of fright." His works, like the works of Gilchrist, invoke mystery because they are about the mystery that borders, and by bordering defines, what we think it is to be human, to be normal. Death, exile, and madness are all ultimate states of non-being that give the shape to our being. They are the black sea that defines our islands of light and life. We experience them only at the very extremes of our lives, as we move from the obvious to the occulted, and it is impossible for us to imagine what that moment of transition will be like: before the transition we are as we have always been; afterwards we are fundamentally different.

Sime, by plumbing the depths of mystery, teases out some thought, some *unheimlich* understanding, of what this transition might be like. As we gaze into Hish's wide-eyed stare we see the abyss that, as Nietzsche warns us, is more than able to gaze back into us.

Sources cited and further reading:

Heneage, Simon, and Henry. Ford. *Sidney Sime: Master of the Mysterious*. London: Thames & Hudson, 1980.

Dunsany, Lord. *The Gods of Pegāna*. London: Elkin Mathews, 1905.

———. *My talks with Dean Spanley*. London: William Heinemann, 1936.

The Sidney Sime Memorial Gallery at Worplesden Memorial Hall http://www.sidneysimegallery.org.uk

Apart from a few pieces held at Worplesden, much of Sime's work is in private hands and is difficult to gain consent for official reproduction. There are good reproductions of Sime's work online, however. Most notable is a lengthy post on John Howe's blog (http://www.john-howe.com/blog/2009/02/15/from- an-ultimate-dim-thule/) and a large collection on the Monster Brains website (http://monsterbrains.blogspot.co.uk/2011/06/sidney-sime. html).

Horrors of the Everyday Life

June Pulliam

Get Out. Jordan Peele, director. Universal, 2017.
American Horror Story: Cult. Brian Falchuck and Ryan Murphy, creators. FX, 2017–18.

It's hard to make horror these days, as zombies, vampires, ghosts, and even the killers of the typical slasher film aren't as frightening as they used to be. Part of the reason that these creatures have a diminished ability to scare lies in their overexposure: audiences are so familiar with these tropes that they have lost their power to shock. But the biggest reason that these old tropes are losing their power to frighten is the zeitgeist of the present day. In a world where mass shootings are the order of the day, where the spate of natural disasters are the most recent signs that our planet will be uninhabitable in the next fifty years, where police walk free after murdering people of color, and where civil discourse is only a distant memory, zombies, ghosts, and vampires don't seem terribly scary. Is it any wonder then that *The Walking Dead* feels like a documentary of the future, since the most frightening monsters of all are fellow humans? The best horror, then, embraces the horror of the present day in a way that re-presents it to the audience in a way that helps them to understand just what the hell is happening. Two standout works this year that deal with the horrors of everyday life are Jordan Peele's film *Get Out* and the most recent installment of Bryan Falchuck and Ryan Murphy's American Horror Story, *Cult*.

Get Out describes the horror of being a person of color in a supposedly post-racist society where all are treated for the quality of their character rather than the color of their skin. In the film's first scene, a dark-skinned African American who is visiting a friend's house for the first time becomes lost in a wealthy white suburb. When the driver of an expensive car slows down to look at the man, he quickly retreats into the shadows lest he become the next Trayvon Martin. Soon after, a figure in armor emerges from the bushes and chloroforms him into unconsciousness before depositing him in the trunk of the car. The rest of the film follows Chris, a black photographer who is taken to meet his girlfriend Rose's wealthy white parents for the first time. But this is not *Guess Who's Coming to Dinner,* and Chris is not Sidney Poitier. During the weekend, Chris becomes increasingly unsettled by Rose's family and their black servants, a maid and gardener who all look and speak as if they had been transported from a 1930s film and taken so many benzos that they have achieved eternal mindfulness. Rose's parents and their friends are even more unsettling. Rose's neurosurgeon father, Dean Armitage, looks like the offspring of Sigmund Freud and Steve Jobs, and his declaration that he would have voted for Obama a third time sounds a bit like the claim that one cannot be racist because of having a black friend. Rose's mother, Missy, is a psychiatrist specializing in using hypnosis to plant suggestions in people that can help them quit smoking or stop resisting when someone is trying to hijack their consciousness. Chris feels particularly conspicuous when he is expected to socialize with the family's friends, as he seems to be the only person of color who is not a servant.

Of course, things are not as they seem. Rose and her family and their friends have sinister intentions toward Chris that go far beyond what his best friend Rod warns of—that the white people are going to kidnap him and turn him into a sex slave. The Armitage family has perfected a technique that can potentially give the privileged few eternal life by putting their brains into the bodies of healthy younger people. Because so many of the Armitages' clients feel that being black is essentially the next big thing, Rose and her brother are tasked with bringing back potential hosts, either through seduction (Rose's preferred method) or brute force (the favored tactic of her brother Jeremy). While much of the host's brain is removed, enough remains so that the personality occasionally resurfaces. In one particularly chilling scene, Chris is outside at night when he spots the family housekeeper/maid Georgina in her bedroom window, staring at her reflecting in the glass and touching her hair, as if everything about herself is terribly unfamiliar to her. The actress who plays Georgina, Sarah Valentine, a mixed-race black woman who was raised by a white family, says in a recent *New York Times* article that this scene where Georgina is struggling with "the white woman inside of her felt chillingly real to" her because it dramatized her own experience "of being internally suppressed by whiteness at the hands of people who are supposed to care about" her.[*] Georgina's experience externalizes the experience racial minorities in a majority white culture, where mainstream success involves a degree of assimilation.

In order to escape the Armitages' compound, Chris must kill the family, and within the frame of the film he seems to be fulfilling all negative stereotypes about black males as hyper-violent. One of the film's final scenes is a visual reference to *Othello,* a text

[*]Nicole Fineman, "Beyond the Scream: What I Learned from Horror Movies," *New York Times* (13 October 2017). Web.

in which a black man is represented as more predisposed to acts of violence against his loved ones than whites.

Director Jordan Peele is particularly aware of what his film communicates about racism in the twenty-first century. In his director's commentary, he explains that the version of *Get Out* shown in theaters was an alternative ending that he thought was necessary after the 2016 elections. Given that the antithesis to Barack Obama now occupies the White House, Peele believed it was necessary to show that his protagonist did not succumb to racist stereotypes about blacks, and so Chris does not have it in him to be Othello, in spite of his girlfriend attempting to enslave him.

American Horror Story: Cult similarly lacks any traditional monsters, even though each season of the show is a bricolage of well-known horror tropes. While Twisty the Clown from *AHS: Freak Show* is back to menace a new generation, *Cult* does not seem to be riffing on *IT,* or even the scary clown trope, for that matter. Instead, *Cult* explores the carnival atmosphere that has taken hold of the United States via the 2016 election. *Cult* mirrors what Mikhail Bakhtin describes as the carnivalesque in *Rabelais and His World*. Features of the carnivalesque include the acceptance of otherwise prohibited behavior and the commingling of people and categories that are normally separated. Though he is not a character in the show, the Orange POTUS is the Lord of Misrule presiding over the carnival of fury that erupts in the first episode of *Cult* after his election. Kai Anderson (Evan Peters) celebrates Trump's victory on election night because it means that he is now free to seed dissent and bring together Bernie and Hillary supporters with Red Hats to burn to the ground democratic institutions that both see as fundamentally oppressive.

Episode 5, "Mid-Western Assassin," was so prescient that FX edited the aired version to avoid unsettling viewers just days after Stephen Paddock killed 58 and wounded 546 in Las Vegas in the bloodiest mass shooting in recent United States history. In the opening and unedited scene of the streaming version, the sight of people cowering in terror as a lone gunman picks off people in the crowd was already familiar to viewers, who earlier in the week had seen similar footage shot from the cell phones of terrified people in a Las Vegas plaza. But the events depicted in this episode are not that of a lone madman, but instead, one carefully orchestrated by Kai and his band of Juggalos that the most hard-core, tinfoil-hatted conspiracy theorist would love.

A Century Too Late

Tony Fonseca

SAM GAFFORD. *The Dreamer in Fire and Other Stories*. New York: Hippocampus Press, 2017. 244 pp. $20.00. tpb. ISBN: 9781614981954.

Sam Gafford's *The Dreamer in Fire and Other Stories* is yet another collection of Lovecraftian–Cthulhuvian tales, and while these might be fighting words in some quarters, I feel that someone needs to say it: Do we really need more stories of the Old Ones and Lovecraftian dark gods who exist on the periphery of human imagination? Lovecraft's stories were outré when they were published, but any fictional myth can be new for only so long, and the opposite of new in fiction is stale, stagnant, and unimaginative. In some ways, then, this review is unfair to Gafford, who is by all rights an engaging writer in his technique and mastery of dialogue. In fact, some of the tales in this collection are rather good. Readers will enjoy "Homecoming," although some may question how any story can end with unstoppable monsters being easily stopped, even if briefly. Such problems can make tales only so good.

The bottom line is that by 2017, authors should have lain Lovecraft's monsters to rest and moved on to horrors of their own making, instead of toying with the idea that the Old Ones can be updated to fit our times. The tale "Casting Fractals" attempts this, and to be blunt, if the reader were to replace the 1960s reporter with a late 1920s reporter and simply change the historical events he references to events contemporary, it would be the same story, with the same tale within a tale structure, with the same Lovecraftian curious narrator who stumbles on someone's papers to find out that the gods are lovers of chaos and destruction, bent on the enslavement and destruction of this puny race of creatures called humanity. In short, stories that resurrect the same monsters, with the same themes, following the same convention and rules, can go only so far until they become ridiculous, no matter how sublime in their original vision.

To put it another way, Gafford here is playing literary Sisyphus, pushing one story after another up a hill only to have it roll down to an inexorable conclusion because the rules are established, have been established since the 1920s. In addition, any contemporary author writing Lovecraftian fiction can only pale in comparison to the original creator in technique, vision, and execution. Moreover, that author is now tasked with finding something new under the sun (or in the dark recesses where the sun doesn't shine), an impossible task. In this particular case, Gafford does himself a disservice. He captures the Lovecraftian ethos well, as in this passage from "Showtime," a possession tale about a children's television performer who has been turned into a mouthpiece for the Lords of Chaos:

> Banks looked into my eyes and I saw, for the briefest instant, what he had seen. It was the future. The earth had been wiped clean, and huge, hideous things slid and climbed over the wreckage of humanity. Dark horrors swam through the air and reached through the clouds. . . . And over it all, orchestrating the terror, was Azathoth. The Lord of Chaos ululated grotesquely over the cosmos.

Granted, this is good prose, and it was good prose when Lovecraft wrote it almost a century ago.

And unfortunately, because all the stories must be narrated in Lovecraftian fashion and end on an ominous note, Gafford has to orchestrate events so much that they seem contrived. In "Showtime," a flippant final statement that "you just can't beat good TV" is a nice attempt at cynicism, but it falls flat because, well, nowhere in the story are readers ever shown an example of the must-see Cthulhuvian TV program to which children are being subjected. This is a shame on many fronts, because such scenes would have been infinitely creepy, but more importantly, they would have made the narrator's final statement make sense, rather than come across as a generalized cynical statement. A similar problem occurs in "Casting Fractals," where the narrator, who has gone through great trouble to save a box of papers that belonged to his idol (a veteran reporter who through his investigations has seen the other side, become an alcoholic, and retired from life), and who has gone to the trouble of finding his idol and meeting with him, would suddenly forget to turn over the box of papers he has been saving for *just such an occasion*. But Gafford has to contrive this forgetfulness so that the narrator can do what Lovecraftian narrators do, rummage through the box in private and become the newly cursed human who can see the gods on the periphery.

Other stories in the collection succeed or fail to various degrees. "Homecoming" makes such good use of gore and implied threat that it succeeds admirably (until its aforementioned ending). A study in the dark recesses of the mind, it posits a world where a stepfather is manipulated by the gods into raping and murdering his sixteen-year-old stepdaughter so that she can become possessed and return from the dead; in addition, it has some nice twists, although a bit more exploration into exactly how the narrator fits into the Lords of Chaos's grand scheme is needed, since his useful idiocy is established. But readers are left to wonder why he is allowed to live imprisoned for murder after ostensibly halting Yog-Sothoth's plan with a simple axe (was there no lawnmower available?). But why? Is he being allowed to watch the world die from a cell? Is his punishment the knowledge that he killed his wife and children to no avail? Readers are left in the lurch. The story would have been much more threatening had the narrator stopped to think about these deeper issues—thereby introducing them into the narration in a logical way that would make the ending clear.

On the opposite end of the spectrum are tales like "The Adventure of the Prometheus Calculation." In it, Sherlock Holmes is a robot who suddenly decides he wants to solve the mystery of his creator. As predictable as this is, even more predictable is that, of course, his creator is Moriarty. And, of course, the story has to end with both detective-bot and creator disappearing after Moriarty makes a predictably impassioned speech about his progeny's turning on him (and Mary Shelley sighs in her grave). When a reader can write the story in his/her mind after two pages, this is a sign that the writer is either unimaginative or, as I believe in this case, being hemmed in by genre (or in this case subgenre) convention. A Lovecraftian story has to be, well, Lovecraftian, meaning that such stories become write-by-number affairs. Such is the nature of writing stories to fit a mold—any mold, including lofty Lovecraftian homage. But the bottom line is that I feel for these authors; like those Lovecraftian narrators in those tales within tales, they are doomed at the start, in their case by the dark gods of convention, the moment they type the first letter of the first story.

Standing Behind the Curtains:
A Conversation with T. E. D. Klein

Barry Lee Dejasu

[This interview originally appeared in the final issue of *Shock Totem* magazine and has been graciously shared with *Dead Reckonings*.]

In the early 1980s, horror fiction had reached a wider audience than ever before. Authors such as Peter Straub, Clive Barker, Ramsey Campbell, and, of course, Stephen King raised the standards of writing quality, deftly scaling the summits of popularity and bringing the genre to a new level of literary appreciation. Among their ranks was a writer named T. E. D. Klein, who would ultimately become one of the most important voices in modern horror fiction.

Theodore Donald Klein (the "E" stands for "Eibon," a literary reference to Clark Ashton Smith's Hyperborean sorcerer) was born and raised in New York. A graduate of Brown University, Klein would later study at Columbia, which led to a stint in the late 1970s at Paramount as a script reader. In 1981, he became the founding editor of the highly acclaimed *Rod Serling's Twilight Zone Magazine,* publishing works by authors such as Stephen King, Peter Straub, and Harlan Ellison before parting ways in 1985.

In 1984, Klein published his first, and so far only, novel, *The Ceremonies*. An expansion of an earlier novella named "The Events at Poroth Farm" (itself in turn inspired by "The White People," a classic short story by Welsh dark fantasy author Arthur Machen), *The Ceremonies* was an excursion into cosmic horror set against the backdrop of contemporary American culture. *The Ceremonies* enjoyed a brief ride on the *New York Times* bestseller list, and although it's now long out of print, it is considered a classic.

The following year, Klein released a collection of four novellas, known as *Dark Gods*. Although three of its novellas were previously published elsewhere (one in Kirby McCauley's legendary 1980 anthology *Dark Forces*), one of them, "Nadelman's God," was original to the collection and would subsequently go on to win the 1986 World Fantasy Award for Best Novella. And just like *The Ceremonies, Dark Gods* is unfortunately very much out of print.

As the years went by, Klein would go on to publish fewer than a dozen short stories, most of which (along with "The Events at Poroth Farm") were collected in a 2006 limited-edition book from Subterranean Press, *Reassuring Tales*. As with his previous works, this has unfortunately become an out-of-print rarity, and due to its limited print run (only 600 signed and numbered copies exist), it's even harder to find than the others, often being listed for over $100 in online stores.

Klein may have estranged himself from the genre that he helped shape, but even after nearly three decades his influence has never been forgotten. To date, authors such as Thomas Ligotti, John Langan, Laird Barron, Paul Tremblay, and Simon Strantzas look fondly upon his works as a directly influence upon their own.

In a rare and exclusive gesture, Mr. Klein broke his silence to generously discuss his life, writings, and career.

BLD: While you were growing up, what did you like to read? Who were some authors that you just couldn't get enough of, and not necessarily in horror?

TK: I loved a series of maritime adventure books by Howard Pease (or rather, by one of the authors with that name; there appear to have been two), who wrote about tramp steamers plying the South Seas. As a boy, I used to clip out the daily shipping news from the back of the *Times*—those listings still seem pretty romantic to me—and I imagined, crazily enough, that I would someday ship out on a rusted freighter and visit all sorts of exotic ports of call. Actually, I'm a lousy traveler and have always been afraid of the water.

My favorite childhood book had also been my father's favorite: Booth Tarkington's *Penrod* trilogy, in a thick black omnibus volume with my father's name stamped all over it. It's basically an early-twentieth-century *Tom Sawyer,* albeit a little more domesticated, and the writing's extremely droll. I read the book again and again and still remember many lines from it—like the description of a caterpillar motionless on a twig, looking as if it were "lost in reverie." Two friends from the neighborhood and I were even inspired to form a secret club we called the P.S. of A.P.B. (which stood for "the Penrod and Sam of All Penrod Books").

BLD: Around what age did you become interested in writing? What were some of your earliest writings about?

TK: At a point (probably in junior high), when I had read most of the celebrated Robert Heinlein juveniles and was moving on to the stuff for older readers, I remember getting involved in a writing competition with a brainy friend over who could complete a book first. He was going to write a history of the world (I said he was brainy), and I was going to write a science fiction novel. Neither one of us got very far, but I remember a few things my manuscript contained that, at the time, struck me as extremely neat but may well have been cribbed from things I'd read. I had my hero, a Heinleinesque space cadet, finish his training in a graduation ceremony that ended, symbolically, with each new graduate being shoved off the rostrum into a pit of mud. There was a space-travel scene (also Heinlein-inspired, I'm sure) in which a sleek rocket ship brought travelers up to some sort of giant, drab, ungainly interstellar transport chamber, floating somewhere beyond the moon, inside of which they stood around impatiently like a crowd of commuters in the main hall of Grand Central Station, smoking cigarettes and chatting; and when they filed out a few minutes later, they were at the other end of the galaxy. And there was a time traveler who miscalculated and somehow materialized where a brick wall had once been standing (or would someday be standing), "and before he could be rescued," I wrote, "his heart had turned to cement."

BLD: What about dark fiction appealed to you so much, to read it and to write it?

TK: Well, I think it just makes the world more interesting; [I gather] you mean what's usually described as "supernatural horror." A world with room in it for the supernatural would be both darker and potentially lighter than the one I believe we're actually living in; it would be a world richer in meaning, scarier and yet more charming. On the other hand, if there were even an ounce of religion among the things I happen to believe in (and there isn't), supernatural fiction would probably hold little appeal for me. I'd have no emotional need for it.

As for writing it, I suppose initially there's the normal desire to imitate the authors who've given one pleasure, followed later by the desire to modify, critique, and even poke fun at those same formative figures. (I guess you'd file that under "anxiety of influence.") Plus (and I'm sure this has been said a million times) for anyone who's ever been frightened, as I have, by a scary story or a horror film, there's a certain gratification in creating something of the same sort yourself, where it's you that's standing behind the curtains, controlling the action. It's akin to the reassurance a child may feel when he sees a behind-the-scenes photo of the guy in the rubber monster suit, or learns the secret of how special effects are produced, or gets the autograph, at a horror convention, of some actor who once scared him in the movies.

BLD: It's pretty obvious (from the themes and subject matter of your works) that you were a fan of Lovecraft and Machen. When did you get into them?

TK: I first encountered those writers in the most commonplace, boring old way—by coming across their work at my local library (in that celebrated Modern Library Giant, most likely).[*] Later, at college in Providence, I found myself strolling daily through Lovecraft's beloved old neighborhood, buying Arkham House books at a shop he himself had frequented, and, during my senior year, living next door to a house that figures in "The Call of Cthulhu."

So for a while, I really became quite consumed with HPL—with his life as well as his fiction. Plus I've always had a tremen-

---

[*]*Great Tales of Horror and the Supernatural* (1944), ed. Herbert A. Wise and Phyllis Fraser.

dous fondness for New England, and Lovecraft is surely a key part of that; he's made it (the entire region, crazy as this may sound) a somewhat magical place.

BLD: If you don't mind my asking, which house had you lived in? (I myself am a Providence resident, and was born only a couple of blocks away from Lovecraft's own birthplace.)

TK: It's great that you were born so near HPL's birthplace. That's certainly one of the charms of Providence—feeling that his presence is so close. The house I lived in was the Deacon Edward Taylor House, 9 Thomas Street. I loved that building and felt grateful to be living in it. I remember the third floor, where I lived, had wide plank floorboards (creaking slightly, I think) and fireplaces in all four rooms.

BLD: Were any of your stories, or even *The Ceremonies,* ever optioned for film?

TK: Some blessed person did option *The Ceremonies* a few years ago, but obviously nothing has come of it. And a filmmaker in England has an option on "Children of the Kingdom." I wish him luck.

BLD: How does it feel to know how much your work has been a direct influence upon many established and renowned authors, such as Thomas Ligotti and Laird Barron?

TK: I'm actually astonished to hear that anyone's ever said such a thing; it's news to me. I'm pleased, I guess, but it's awfully hard to imagine anyone being influenced by anything of mine, especially considering how little I've managed to turn out.

BLD: Your work is *very* highly regarded. In fact, you have an entire stretch of a chapter in S. T. Joshi's *The Modern Weird Tale: A Critique of Horror Fiction*, right alongside Shirley Jackson, William Peter Blatty, Stephen King, Clive Barker, Ramsey Campbell, and Robert Bloch.

TK: That sort of thing is always a bit shocking to hear, but very nice, obviously.

BLD: Back in the '80s, you'd announced work on a new novel. Whatever became of that? Did you just never finish it, or is it pending heavy edits and in some sort of hiatus?

TK: Yes, it was going to be called *Nighttown;* it still may be! I got around halfway through, by which time I began to worry that it was getting out of hand; I mean, getting too long and complicated. (I had originally intended it to be a lively, fast-moving read, on the order of *The 39 Steps*, but clearly that sort of thing isn't a natural fit.) And then, unfortunately, I got distracted, which is always a problem. I find writing quite difficult, and I'm good at finding ways to avoid it.

BLD: So what did you end up doing instead? What have you been up to since?

TK: Thanks for asking. Life is definitely full of distractions, if you're looking for them. At one point, in the early '90s, when I should have been hard at work on the new book, I happily spent my time editing a true-crime magazine called *CrimeBeat,* which made a bit of a splash on newsstands but alas ran out of money after fourteen issues; though while it lasted it was great fun and something I'd always wanted to do. (I should add that although it was based on my own proposal, the initial capital was raised by my old mentor from *Twilight Zone,* Eric Protter, who died this past year; as did, more recently, my agent, Kirby McCauley; as did, even more recently, Alice Turner of *Playboy*. All three were friends I was very close to, for decades, and to whom I owe a lot.)

During that same period (this time thanks to Kirby), I also had the chance to write a screenplay for the Italian director Dario Argento, adapted from a treatment of his. The movie itself (*Trauma,* 1983) turned out to be unwatchable; I, at least, have never managed to sit through it. (You know how Machen said something like "I dreamed in fire, but I worked in clay"? He might have been talking about that woeful little film.) Still, it was exciting to work on a script, and actually explore locations, with a colorful, amusing, albeit exasperating character like Argento.

Subsequently I did some teaching at John Jay College, part of the city university system. I enjoyed it. I once spent a year teaching high school English in Dexter, Maine—one of the best years of my life.

For the past decade, I've been working for *GQ;* my official title is senior copy editor. The senior part is appropriate, as I'm probably the oldest guy on the staff. Basically I spend my day inserting and deleting commas; I really know my commas. When I first got the job, my friend Margie said, "What?! You're the most un-*GQ* person I've ever known." I still take that as a compliment. The company, Condé Nast, has just vacated its offices in the heart of Times Square and is now ensconced, for better or worse, in the new World Trade Center downtown. I can't say I'm warming to the place, and I expect to retire soon.

BLD: Would you ever consider returning to writing fiction again?

TK: Definitely, although I have to admit I'm somewhat less interested in horror fiction, and fiction in general, than I used to be; it's probably a consequence of age. I find I prefer to read big fat history books these days, and a smattering of popular science—trying to make up for too many years of ignorance.

BLD: Would you like to say anything to all the authors, artists, etc. who have been inspired by you over the years?

TK: I'm truly grateful, but now please try some good nonfiction!

BLD: Ted, this was a real honor. Thank you so much for your time!

TK: Thank you.

Uncanny Age: Joachim Kalka's Gaslight

James Machin

JOACHIM KALKA. *Gaslight: Lantern Slides from the Nineteenth Century*. Translated by Isabel Fargo Cole. New York: New York Review Books, 2017. 240 pp. $17.95 tpb. ISBN: 978-1-681371-18-4.

Joachim Kalka is a German essayist, literary critic, and a prodigious translator, responsible for German iterations of works by everyone from Christopher Hitchens to Arthur Machen. This collection, *Gaslight,* is subtitled "Lantern Slides from the Nineteenth Century." It makes available to an Anglophone readership a selection of Kalka's essays, all loosely concerned with the question, "does the nineteenth century exist?," meaning: how are we to think of our retroactive constructions of that century and the manner in which it continues to resonate through our present understanding of ourselves? Despite its evocative name, the book has a decidedly larger ambit than the specific concerns of *Dead Reckonings,* though Kalka frequently touches upon the horrific, weird, and the uncanny, and it is on these elements of the collection that I will focus for the purposes of this review.

The thread drawn through across a bewildering variety of literary sources (albeit with a definite European focus) is that of the struggle with modernity, felt across centuries and cultures. This probably makes it sound less fun than it is: I can't comment on how Kalka reads in his native German, but thanks to Isabel Fargo Cole's translation, his prose is consistently fluent and accessible. This despite the fact that Kalka's flights of associative fancy at times leave readers breathless in their attempt to keep up with the pace of his thinking. An essayist in the best sense, Kalka's breadth of reading may be intimidating, but stylistically he is warm, witty, and engaging.

The opening essay, "The True Unity Is Given by the Police," deals with the impact of the police force as a novelty in the early nineteenth century, associated with the rise of the post-industrial metropolis. Kalka highlights the now surprising treatment by Friedrich Schiller of the new surveillance infrastructure as an unambiguous social good; he imbues the police with a sheen of almost metaphysical redemptive power in its pastoral control of society. Naïve, perhaps, but only with the benefit of hindsight: "Schiller's work marks a point at which the police could still be conceived as heroic and full of mystery." Kalka identifies the animus here as one of imposing order on the incoherent jumble of the new urban environment. He next looks at the development of military technology, examining the utopian quest for the "weapon to end all wars": the martial potential of submarines and balloons was the nineteenth-century forerunner to the nuclear deterrent. Here we segue into the "Techno-Romantic-Adventure" of Jules Verne; long before Nemo, the American engineer Robert Fulton "offered the French government plans for a submarine which he called the 'Nautilus,'" which was to "navigate secretly under the hulls of English battleships and plant mines." The notion was rejected by Napoleon for its apparent eccentricity and questionable honor (Fulton duly offered his plans to the British).

After a diverting discussion of Balzac, Kalka turns his attention to the early nineteenth-century culture wars in Germany, discussing the influence of the nationalist literary critic Wolfgang Menzel. Menzel seems to have spent much of his career defining himself and his aspirations for German letters in specific opposition to the "degenerate" Goethe. Interestingly, this adjectival choice of Menzel's here (the German *entartet*) is designated as being "where that peculiar, poisoned word truly seems to start its career." The implication is that Menzel precipitated the notion of degenerate art, degenerate culture, etc., popularized at the end of the nineteenth century by the German critic Max Nordau. The fin-de-siècle anxiety about degeneration underpins most of the prominent horror texts of the period, such as *Dracula,* "The Great God Pan," and *Strange Case of Dr. Jekyll and Mr. Hyde.* Here Kalka roots the notion earlier, in Menzel's era's "intellectual psychopathology," rooted in nationalist insecurity.

Fans of Wagner and those interested in German romanticism generally will find much to appreciate in the discussion of the Ring Cycle in "I Lie in Fetters Forged by Me." In "Max Eyth and the Specter of Technology," Kalka reiterates the underpinning argument of the collection: "We must go back to the nineteenth century to grasp some little part of the chain of unsolved— unsolvable?—problems we drag along behind us, for it is there that everything begins" (*Gaslight* is replete with such arresting Gothic imagery). Through a discussion of the engineering career of Eyth, Kalka casts light on the litany of disasters that accompanied this particularly experimental stage in technological history, arguing that "if literature is any guide, brilliant engineers are far more often dedicated to the craft of destruction than that of construction." From here, it's a short wander into the company of the insane inventors of Jules Verne and H. G. Wells, and the enduring problem of whether "*any* of us, individuals or humanity as a whole, possess anything resembling the ability to keep pace mentally (rationally and emotionally) with the technological capabilities we ourselves have created."

The historical entrenchment of anti-Semitism in both German and French culture is explored in two essays. The latter through a particularly compelling and comprehensive account of the Dreyfus affair, which had such a corrosive effect on French society during the Belle Époque, precipitating a traumatic crisis of national conscience. Kalka reveals the astonishing levels of ambient German anti-Semitism through a survey of nineteenth-century spa culture. An integral part of German spa holidays was communal singing, and the traditional songs were inevitably crudely anti-Semitic. Preposterous enough as this sounds, Kalka neatly reveals the substrata of anxieties at work here; national identity, cultural "purity," and the crucial role of scapegoating in the contrivance of ersatz communal spirit. These grotesque spa songs were disseminated through "jolly" postcards home, and Kalka is unflinching in his analysis of German anti-Semitism "as a type of pathology," a "toxic monomania" which also found expression through a cottage industry of conspiracy theory (if only this too remained a recondite footnote of history, along with the spa souvenir cards).

Talking of "toxic monomania," perhaps most of interest to readers of *Dead Reckonings* will be the essay "Gaslight, Fog, Jack the Ripper," within which Kalka comprehensively exposes the vacuity of Patricia Cornwell's obsession with convicting the artist Walter Sickert as the Whitechapel fiend, against all evidence and sense (depressingly, Cornwell has now added gratuitous vandalism of his paintings to her CV). Kalka's focus, however, is the interplay between gaslight and fog, the comforting and the uncanny, that still steeps our collective memory of the period. As well as the more obvious referents such as Dickens and the Sherlock Holmes stories, Kalka turns to Machen's "The Great God Pan" to explore how "gas lighting becomes the signature of an era—or rather a cipher of our mythical remembrance of a historical period." G. K. Chesterton's superbly weird (and, in my opinion, underrated, or at least overlooked) novella *The Man Who*

Was Thursday (1908) is also given some deserved attention, as it is elsewhere in the book.

The essay "The Bomb: What a Beautiful Breach in the World" is one of the most bravura in the collection. Taking as his starting point the fin-de-siècle enthusiasm for dynamite as a tool of terrorism, fueled by nascent anarchist and nihilist ideologies (as well, of course, as having only recently been made possible by Nobel's invention), Kalka moves from the nothingness at the center of the dynamite explosion to the use of absence in literature. He identifies this void as a topos of a range of genres, from dirty jokes to mystery fiction and the ghost story. The absence at the heart of the literary mystery is linked to the nihilistic void of explosive destruction represented in several notable works of the period, for example Stevenson's *The Dynamiter* and Conrad's *The Secret Agent*. Whereas the Victorian detective can operate as a "curative force," fixing such breaches in our understanding of the world, "the explosion of the nihilist bomb, with its new logic, is irreversible."

Apropos of Patrick Hamilton's 1938 play *Gaslight,* Kalka explains the tendrils of Victorian fog lingering over contemporary culture thus:

> We still enjoy subjecting ourselves for a while to the feeling that "strangers have entered the house," but we also long for the long-lost assurance that nothing will befall us, that, in the end the light will burn calmly once again. The present has long since ceased to offer any guarantee of that. The gaslight glows across to us with the strangely nebulous nimbus of an uncanny age that—long ago—promised security all the same.

Kalka's *Gaslight,* as a whole, is a hugely erudite peregrination through this "uncanny age."

A Mixed Bag

S. T. Joshi

JUSTIN STEELE and SAM COWAN, ed. *Looming Low, Volume 1.*
Carmichael, CA: Dim Shores, 2017. 338 pp. $50.00 (deluxe hc);
$18.00 (tpb). ISBN: 978-0-9991430-4-9.

This bulky volume comes with a great many advance plaudits,
mostly from the authors included in it; but there is reason to
doubt whether it is the be-all and end-all of contemporary weird
anthologies.

There is, at the very outset, a lack of clarity as to what this
book is actually meant to achieve. The chief editor, the young
Justin Steele, writes: "The twenty-six stories in this anthology
were selected by Sam and I [*sic*] to give readers a look at some of
the brightest voices in weird fiction today." Well, that's a pretty
broad purview. I am far from being an advocate of "theme" anthologies, for in a distressing number of cases the volume's
"theme" is so narrow and artificial that it causes its lugubrious
authors to turn all manner of somersaults in accommodating
their ideas to it. But if *Looming Low, Volume 1* presents itself as
widely representative of contemporary weird fiction, then questions immediately arise as to the choice of authors—who was selected and who was *not* selected.

I suppose it is unreasonable to expect a relatively new press to
have sufficient prestige (and a sufficient budget) to attract such
veterans as Ramsey Campbell, Peter Straub, Thomas Ligotti, or
Steve Rasnic Tem; but why are other, younger writers of prominence not included? Where is Caitlín R. Kiernan, undeniably the
leading weird writer of her generation? Where are Nancy Kilpat-
rick, Elizabeth Hand, Jonathan Thomas, John Langan, Kelly Link,
Reggie Oliver, Jason V Brock, and others one could mention? (I
am surprised that Steele—whose sole previous editorial credit is a
volume of stories in tribute to Laird Barron—was unable to get
Barron to contribute anything.)

As it is, *Looming Low* includes, among its twenty-six authors, only five who have genuine prominence in the field: Michael Cisco, Gemma Files, Richard Gavin, Simon Strantzas, and Jeffrey Thomas. This is not to say that lesser-known writers cannot do good work; indeed, it will become apparent that such writers have written several of the better stories in the book. But one begins to wonder whether the editors simply contacted their limited cadre of friends and said, "Write me something weird," without making any comprehensive effort to canvass the entire range of contemporary weird writing.

A book, of course, must be judged on what it has, not on what it does not have. But even by this standard, *Looming Low* comes up a bit short. I am sorry to report that the number of poor or mediocre stories substantially outweighs the number of meritorious ones. Some stories are poorly written; others are poorly executed; some are too short (i.e., do not adequately convey their core ideas); some are too long. The editors should have sent a good number of stories back to their authors for revision, and should simply have rejected others.

In particular, the key element of weird writing—the symbolic function of the supernatural—is bungled in story after story. In non-mimetic stories, the supernatural serves as a metaphor for central human concerns in a manner that can be more vivid and memorable than in mimetic fiction; but it all depends on the exact role and function of the supernatural in the story in question.

Consider the opening story in the book, Kurt Fawver's "The Convexity of Our Youth." This long-winded account of an orange ball that causes strange illnesses in children, who become balls themselves, is confused in its very essence because the symbolism of children becoming balls is never clarified. Why orange balls (which apparently resemble basketballs) and not something else? Fawver is apparently intending some kind of satire on middle-class life, but the story collapses of its own incoherence.

This same problem besets Damien Angelica Walters's "The Unquiet Space." Here the supernatural element is an anomalous spot that appears on the wall of a house and resists being painted over. A woman named Bailey is concerned that the spot is somehow dangerous, but her husband, Cal (who is fighting alcoholism), discounts the idea. Nevertheless, when he punches a hole in the wall where the spot is, there is revealed something that looks like a "vertical pool of watered milk." What is this—and the stain itself—meant to signify? The reader never knows; and the story is also narrated in a flat, affectless manner that fails to engender the reader's interest.

In Kristi DeMeester's "The Small Deaths of Skin and Plastic," a woman is constantly giving birth to strange babies, apparently made of hard plastic. They are all taken away by the doctors who tend to her, and who apparently keep her confined to her hospital bed. But the story raises many questions that remain unanswered: How did the woman get this way? what is the exact purport of plastic babies? why do the doctors, at one point, attach their mouths to the babies? What, in general, is the *point* of this story?

In contrast, Lucy A. Snyder's "That Which Does Not Kill You" does use the supernatural effectively as a symbol. Here a woman, Emily, wakes up with a horrible pain in her chest: she finds that her heart is missing. She sees her longtime lover, Ashley, packing up her things: she is moving in with a new lover, a man named Kurt. Here the symbolism of the missing heart (as representing the collapse of a relationship) is perhaps excessively obvious, but is nonetheless powerfully handled.

Other stories are spoiled by a failure to develop their ideas adequately. Daniel Mills's "The Christiansen Deaths" is the story of the life and death of a married couple, Lars and Sigrid Christiansen, as told by various people who knew them. In the course of the tale we are evidently to infer that Sigrid gave birth to some hideous monster, and that Lars may have somehow taken this creature into himself. The premise is of some interest, but it is not worked out well. Anya Martin's "Boisea trivittata" tells of a woman who finds her house besieged by insects called boxelder bugs. Since they are generally harmless, the woman does not wish to kill them; instead, she attempts to capture them and put them outside. But the bugs keep on coming in greater and greater numbers. Martin is apparently seeking to create a sense of cumulative horror, but the uniformly bland narrative tone she adopts militates against any genuine engagement on the reader's part.

Then there is S. P. Miskowski's "Alligator Point," a lackluster tale of a woman taking her twin daughters camping, in the course of which we are given not so subtle hints that the woman has murdered her husband. Jeffrey Thomas's "Stranger in the House" is the account of an aging man who reflects sadly on the departure of his wife after many years of marriage and the fact that his mother is descending into dementia, failing to recognize him. Then the man himself finds that his own memory—of his wife, his mother, his co-workers, and even himself—is slipping away. Again an interesting premise, but again not narrated in a sufficiently compelling manner. The very next story in the book, Christopher Slatsky's "SPARAGMOS," is similar, dealing at tedious length about a man fearing he is losing his mind.

Michael Griffin's "The Sound of Black Dissects the Sun" is one of the longest stories in the book—and one of the most disappointing. It tells of one Michael Lamassus, who runs the record label Nocturne Musics. He receives in the mail a CD that contains bizarre music that causes him to hallucinate about floating in a subterranean lake. The CD was made by a man named Mitsuko, who has a strong interest in the occult. Lamassus thinks that the release of the CD would "drop a cultural bomb on the world." Somehow Lamassus makes his way to Mitsuko's studio, but finds the musician burnt to a crisp. Once again, there are interesting ideas in this tale—but it is massively, painfully verbose, with long, tiresome accounts of how each track of the CD affects Lamassus, and whines on his part about the decline of the music industry. Griffin is gifted with a fine prose style, but needs to exercise better critical judgment if he is to write an engaging story.

The succession of mediocrities continues. A. C. Wise's "The Stories We Tell about Ghosts" is about teenagers who play a game using a phone app called Ghost Hunt! The narrator is a girl whose younger brother, Gen, is becoming increasingly frightened as the kids go from one purportedly haunted house to another. The story is well written (aside from the author's persistent and unrepentant use of "like" for "as" or "as if" ["his heels [were] hanging over the top step like he was about to do a back flip"]), but the ending is entirely predictable. Brian Evenson's "The Second Door" is a poorly written tale set in a never-never-land where a brother begins to suspect that his sister, who has begun speaking in a non-human tongue, has been replaced by an alien entity. Michael Cisco's "Rock n' [*sic*] Roll Death Squad" is a somewhat opaque series of ruminations by a retired contract killer. This story is luminously transparent in comparison to Lisa L.

Hannett's completely incomprehensible "Outside, a Drifter."

Michael Wehunt's "In Canada" is a standard unreliable-narrator story of a possibly autistic young man who takes refuge in putting on masks of animals and thinking he has become the animal in question. This story is no more than adequate. Slightly less so is Nadia Bulkin's "Live Through This," about a high school student, Danielle Haas, who killed herself after being raped by two of her classmates, and who resurrects herself and kills random members of the community. Bulkin apparently is seeking to mingle black humor and horror, but neither element comes off very well.

There are a few successes in *Looming Low,* although none of these is unequivocal. My personal favorite is perhaps Simon Strantzas's "Doused by Night," a magnificent tale of existential horror. Here the narrator, Miles (possibly an alcoholic), wakes up in a hospital with a strange mark behind his right ear; a doctor harrowingly notifies him that a dozen people have previously been seen with that mark, and they have all died within twenty-four hours. This sets the narrator and his wife on a hunt for the bar where Miles had apparently been the night before. The tale develops a powerful sense of cumulative terror, but is marred by a disappointingly opaque and inconclusive ending.

Strantzas's Canadian colleague Richard Gavin contributes "Banishments," about two brothers who find an iron box floating in a creek. Opening it, they are horrified to find what looks like a baby, not quite human in appearance—but it is made of wax. This tale also gains cumulative strength as it proceeds, even if it is not entirely coherent. Betty Rocksteady's "Dusk Urchin" is a gripping account of a woman whose neighbor, aged about seventy, states that a little girl (aged about ten) has shown up claiming to be his daughter. The neighbor then says he actually killed the girl, but she came back to life. The "child as villain" motif is an old standby in weird fiction (just think of Ray Bradbury's "The Small Assassin"), but here it is handled more than ably.

Livia Llewellyn's "The Gin House, 1935" is a kind of extended prose-poem, as a woman born in the later nineteenth century reflects on her long life of crime and immorality. Llewellyn writes gorgeously evocative prose, but the story is somewhat formless and unfocused. The author also lapses into the error of using "lay" for "lie." Scott Nicolay's "When the Blue Sky Breaks" is really more of a sketch or vignette than a story, as it tells of a teenager girl impregnated by her mother's boyfriend. There are some fine moments of prose-poetry here, but to my mind the story is not genuinely weird—unless one assumes that the author is making faint allusions to Machen's "The White People."

Craig Laurence Gidney's "Mirror Bias" attempts a fusion of sex and weirdness—a dangerous combination that can easily lead to disaster, but one that Gidney manages to pull off creditably. A middle-aged gay man, Percy, communicates on a dating app called Mirror-Bias [sic] with what appears to be a statuesque and well-endowed black man. Does this man really exist? Apparently he does, as he comes through Percy's bathroom mirror for an encounter. The story concludes in a manner not fit to be described in a wholesome family journal like this one; but this ending is effective both erotically and horrifically. Gidney, however, has a somewhat precarious relationship with the English language: he writes "lightening" when he means "lightning," and "san serif" when he means "sans serif"; at one point his protagonist writes of "his parent's [sic] house," which would mean he had only one parent.

Sunny Moraine's "We Grope Together, and Avoid Speech" is an intriguing rumination on the proposition that "There are mouths in the walls." The story gains cumulative strength in only a few pages. Brooke Warra's "Heirloom" is about twin (perhaps Siamese) sisters who are inexorably fused psychologically. The author deftly suggests parallels between their fate and that of rose bushes. Kaaron Warren's "We Are All Bone Inside" is a meandering but nonetheless riveting story about a distinguished family named Naskin, some of whose members are forced to live underground. When an elderly member of the family, Seth, wishes to lay eyes on his sister, Moira, whom he has not seen in sixty years, he enlists the help of his niece, Emily, who ventures underground to find her. I am not entirely sure this story "makes sense" in any orthodox manner, but it is striking and effective.

Looming Low concludes with a lengthy story by Gemma Files, who can always be relied on to deliver. "Distant Dark Places" is a tad long-winded, but tells the mesmerizing story of a woman, Sidonia, who wishes to find her (female) lover, Jong, who has disappeared. Jong is apparently a physicist or astronomer, but she seems to have joined an apocalyptic cult, the Theia Collect, that adheres to a strange hypothesis about how the moon separated from the earth. The tale takes us to a remote part of northern Ontario, where Sidonia and Jong have a dramatic confrontation. While not entirely convincing, the tale's cosmic conclusion is immensely compelling.

I do not know what it will take for editors and publishers in this field to recognize the value of good copy editing. I have already pointed out infelicities in some of the stories; but the problems are far more widespread than that, such as having people speak in numbers (in dialogue a character does not say "10,000" but "ten thousand"). Evidently the publisher did not see fit to hire a capable copyeditor, assuming any was hired at all. The result is a bushel of tiny but annoying imperfections that cumulatively make this anthology significantly poorer than it could have been.

It should be evident from this that *Looming Low* is quite a mixed bag. I truly wish it was better than it is. The editors' inexperience—and perhaps their fear of rejecting, or even of asking for revisions in, stories by their friends may have hampered them. Whatever the case, I hope that in Volume 2 the editors make a more exhaustive attempt to solicit contributions from a wider range of writers, so that that book can be more representative of the best in our field than this one is. There are many fine writers in contemporary weird fiction, and they all need venues for the dissemination of their distinctive output.

The Art of NecronomiCon

Dean Kuhta

I had the honor of participating as a vendor and gallery artist during the 2017 NecronomiCon and Ars Necronomica. Although I had two pieces on display at the gallery show for the 2013 NecronomiCon, this year would be even more exciting for me because I was able to be in attendance. When August had finally arrived, I gathered together my drawings and books and ventured through the rolling hills of New England to the haunted corners and courtyards of Providence, Rhode Island. Upon my arrival during an eldritch and gibbous moon, I methodically set up a web-covered vendor table to display my disturbingly whimsical and grim illustrations. It was also the very first venue that I showcased my new novel, *Silvarum*.

In short, the overall experience was amazing. I had the opportunity to make new friends and reunite with old ones. Most importantly, the NecronomiCon allowed me to be exposed to many other extremely talented artists and writers. Although I have retained many fond memories of the show, there was one in particular that served as the focal point and essence of all that is wonderful about bringing artists together.

There were two original drawings that I had on display at my vendor table. One was a pencil and charcoal drawing called "At the Mountains of Madness" and the other was a large ink illustration entitled "Kadiaphonek." The latter depicted a massive cityscape, filled with curiously angled streets and avenues. It was also saturated in immense detail. Cobblestone streets, layered roof tiles, and double-paned windows stretched and curved throughout the composition. In contrast to the obscene architecture and intersecting lines, the bizarre inhabitants of this city consisted of flying reptiles, crawling insects, and dinosaurs. The combination of all the intense detail and movement created a type of hazy grayness amidst the crosshatching and shading. Although it is difficult to visualize in the scanned version, in the original drawing there are hints of variations in the ink pens I used. Specifically, there are a few areas where the black ink seems to be slightly reddish or pink. Having spent roughly forty hours drawing the piece and staring at every little detail for days, I was of course aware of the discrepancy. The differences in tones were due to the fact that, because the drawing is so enormous, I had run out of my favorite ink pens on numerous occasions. On one such trip to my neighborhood art store, I discovered to my dismay that they were sold out. I grabbed the next best thing and scrambled back to my drawing table.

During the second day of NecronomiCon, one astute individual named Will pointed out these tone variations and asked me what they were all about. I proceeded to explain to him the fantastic tale that I have just shared with you. The moment that stuck with me was when another person was inspecting the same illustration later that day. Will and his wife strolled by my table once again and proceeded to explain to the other person why there were inconsistencies in the black ink. I didn't utter a single word. I just stood there and grinned and appreciated the fact that a group of complete strangers were discussing a technical issue I had had while creating a drawing years ago. That minor glitch had now manifested itself into a real-life event among other people.

To me, that is what art is all about.

Ghosts, Beyond Metaphor and Psychopathology

Jim Rockhill

ZÖE LEHMANN IMFIELD. *The Victorian Ghost Story and Theology: From Le Fanu to James.* New York: Palgrave Macmillan, 2016. 188 pp. $99.99 hc, $79.99 eBook. ISBN: 978-3-319-30218-8.

Dr. Zöe Lehmann Imfield, Lecturer in English Literature at the University of Bern in Switzerland, combined her undergraduate studies in theology and literature for a doctoral thesis on theology in the ghost story before co-editing *Theology and Literature After Postmodernity* (Bloomsbury Publishing, 2015) and adding the current volume to Palgrave Macmillan's series of explorations into the finer details of Gothic and supernatural literature. She is thus the perfect candidate to approach the Gordian knot that typifies the treatment of supernatural elements in British fiction from the second half of the nineteenth century into opening decade of the twentieth, as well as the complex responses these works have elicited from modern readers.

Citing critics like Timothy Larsen (*Contested Christianity: The Political and Social Contexts of Victorian Theology*) and James C. Livingston (*Religious Thought in the Victorian Age: Challenges and Reconceptions*), Dr. Lehmann Imfield postulates that "ghost stories responded not only to a theological conversation in which faith was undermined by skepticism, but to one in which challenges to Christian orthodoxy demanded reinvention and re-engagement with faith," i.e., an engagement with faith closer to

Tennyson's *In Memoriam* ("There lives more faith in honest doubt, / Believe me, than in half the creeds") than to Matthew Arnold's despair at the withdrawing shoreline of the Sea of Faith in "Dover Beach." In her view, "ghost fiction, just as much as 'ghost fact,' was haunted by the uneasy hope that behind Victorian empiricism lay the promise of revelation, and it is the nature of Victorian ghostly discourse which lends the sense of unease." As she interprets the works discussed, all the stories "engage both with the anxieties of faith and doubt, and offer potential models of resolution even when that resolution is not offered to the characters."

The author begins to separate modern perceptions of Victorian ghosts as mere metaphors or symbols of psychological states with a discussion of George Eliot's "The Lifted Veil" (1859), before stating her aim to "challenge the presumption that the supernatural tale lifts a veil only to a void, absent of theological ontology." She means, thereby, to "place the theological import of the supernatural tale alongside that of the gothic and the grotesque in fiction" as a quality that deserves respect rather than a jejune limitation deserving scorn. Chapter 2 "Haunted by the Ghost of God—Reading Theologically," then goes into great, sometimes arcane, detail employing distinctions between theological and teleological; possibility and actuality; narrative and meta-narrative; natural, super-natural and ultra-natural to establish an "'in-between' space of participatory reading" whereby a modern reader can "recover a metaphysical language that currently haunts the discipline of literature as a secular task," and thus appreciate the theological import of these stories without their skepticism "exiling" them the status of what Northrop Frye's *Anatomy of Criticism* (1957) calls "low-mimetic conventions."

Although she also discusses stories by Eliot and May Sinclair, her primary focus is on the work of four "middle-class, middle-aged men," noting that "while all four of the authors considered in this book can make claim as being figures of great influence in the genre," her intent is to use them to "describe a way of reading the texts theologically which sees the approach as being hospitable to other texts and theological perspectives" and to "expand the historical reconsideration of Victorian theological discourse in order to rediscover the theological language of the tales for today's readers." Furthermore, these four authors are particularly valuable to an introductory study of this kind, because each of them approached the supernatural "from very different theological backgrounds and perspectives."

Three of these men were the sons of clergymen, though their religious inclinations were quite different. Joseph Sheridan Le Fanu was of French Huguenot stock, attracted to the theology of Emanuel Swedenborg, and both sympathetic to and repelled by the "superstition" of his Catholic Irish countrymen. Arthur Machen evinced a mystical respect for Anglo-Catholicism and grew up in a rural region of Wales with strong historical ties to the pagan Roman past. As biblical historian and administrator, most of M. R. James's work focuses on the literature and artifacts of the medieval church. Unlike the others, Henry James was the son not of a clergyman but of a Swedenborgian theologian and the brother of the philosopher, psychologist, and investigator of spiritualism William James.

Presented with paradoxes in the fiction and between the fiction and lives of each of these men, Lehmann Imfield lays out a path—that "'in between' space" mentioned earlier—which reconciles these contradictions in terms of the theological reading she posits.

In Machen she sees not a sharp divide between the Decadence of the early stories and the spiritual ecstasy demonstrated in *The Secret Glory*, but a continuity with a change in focus, so that "the pervading sense of 'evil' . . . is one of absence—an absence of soul [Helen in 'The Great God Pan'], an absence of teleological direction [Julian in *The Hill of Souls*]." Thus, "the *absolute* aestheticism portrayed in *The Three Impostors* is the cauldron of evil because it is an aesthetic construct of mystery without a theist understanding of the self in respect to that mystery." In the dark early works exploring "nihilism of being without divine creation, or rather, the non-being of profane creation," agents of "evil" such as the impostors in this episodic novel or the nurse in "The White People" reveal "the paradoxical nature of fallen man," for whom "cathartic religious experience can only occur after paralyzing horror."

The contradictions in the works of M. R. James, the author feels, are due to the failure of most readers (and many of his biographers) to read his ghost stories and his scholarly work as complementary, rather than compartmentalized, portions of a larger oeuvre. She finds it significant that James's extensive scholarly work focuses within the orthodox texts and iconography of the medieval Christian church, its apocrypha, and its heresies: "MRJ the Cambridge scholar, with his fascination with religious texts and 'Truth' through careful tradition, is inextricable from MRJ the ghost-story writer." In this interpretation, the fate of Wraxall in "Count Magnus" and others is not akin to that of Lovecraft's Charles Dexter Ward, whose claim, "I have brought to light a monstrous abnormality, but I did it for the sake of knowledge," strikes us as worthy of our pity. As Lehmann Imfield argues, James interprets knowledge for the sake of knowledge not as a noble pursuit, but as one of Faustian folly, as empty as the writers dissenting from the orthodox views of the early church or Machen's non-beings of profane creation: "it is ultimately not *what* lies outside the Christian concept of the world which provides the terror of MRJ's tales, but the way in which man encounters that world when he views it without the clarifying and redemptive lens of Christian orthodoxy." Knowledge of this kind mimics the truth and misleads mankind; it is a caricature of the truth, just as MRJ's demons caricature the human shape.

Lehmann Imfield intentionally discusses Le Fanu out of sequence, because she interprets the way he handles the paradoxes within the Protestant tradition and his ambivalent treatment of Catholicism as containing "the seeds of a theological reconciliation" based on Le Fanu's ability to "create space, in which man's condition as both fallen and saved can be played out." This chapter is as interesting as the others, but I believe it is less successful than those on Machen, M. R. James, and Henry James for two reasons: at moments it resorts to a more extensive use of specialized jargon similar to that found in Chapter 2, and she relegates discussion of Le Fanu's employment of Swedenborgian themes to the strictly allegorical use of them in "The Mysterious Lodger," deigning not to discuss works such as "Green Tea" and "Squire Toby's Will," which fit less easily with the Augustinian orthodoxy she consistently applies. Nonetheless, insights abound. In the complex novella "The Haunted Baronet," with its doubles, its partial resurrection of one man into another empowered but also overshadowed by his ancestry, and the atonement through death of his one-time oppressor, she sees a journey from horrified aversion to terrified acceptance to redemption through faith, which, while it destroys the present generation, confers a communal sense of grace that results in setting right an ancient wrong between two families. She then compares that problematical allegory "The Mysterious Lodger" with "The Watcher/The Familiar" pointing to them both as reflections of the Book of Job, "in which God himself presents man with situations of absolute despair in order that he will turn to Christ," resulting in a vivid "sense of terror as the catalyst for salvation" that fails to reach a truly convincing sense of fulfillment in the tale of the Lodger, but gives a more hopeful cast to Captain Barton's tribulations, in terms of eternity, than is usually accorded that victim of The Watcher.

The theology that revealed an alternative to nihilism in Machen, quasi-human manifestations dwelling outside the state of grace in M. R. James, and a pathway to redemption through terror in Le Fanu fails in the stories by Henry James examined in Chapter 6. Lehmann Imfield accurately summarizes "The Beast in the Jungle" as "a tale in which the supernatural haunts by its absence," in which the anticipation of astonishment crowds out the ability to recognize and be receptive to the connections that make its proximity felt. She characterizes James's characters as static and paralyzed, his fiction permeated by a "sustained secularism" that refuses to "reflect either the spiritual empiricism of his brother or the mystic faith of his father." The *movement* of the characters toward or away from spiritual danger present in the other works described is conspicuously absent in these works by James. Thus, in "The Altar of the Dead" Stransom not only creates a secular altar in which he alone decides who is worthy of remembrance, but risks alienating his only friend due to his self-absorption. He has stifled receptivity to communication with another, even in church, and even in the presence of the spirit of his dead fiancée. These are characters incapable of redemption, because they are incapable not merely of receiving agape, "the love of God for man and man for God," but even of love for those human beings closest to them. In contrast to May Sinclair's "Where Their Fire Is Not Quenched," where the offer of love is misused and leads to consequences that extend into eternity, these "spiritual tragedies" by James offer "no redemptive or reconciliatory conclusion because the realization is not that a gift" has been offered, but that the characters are incapable of accepting a gift "they have *already refused.*"

The final chapter brings the book back to matters of reader response, and the ways in which the secular reader can read the theological elements implicit in the Victorian ghost story. "The supernatural tale as theological experience is a moment of suspension expanded into a journey, along which travel both the protagonist and the reader." This book helps bring the reader closer to the path that journey follows.

It is unfortunate that the scope of this review merely permitted me to scratch the surface of a supremely thought-provoking book, which, despite some reservations I had in respect to the use of specialized jargon and her underestimating the ingenuity with which Le Fanu uses Swedenborgian themes, I highly recommend to anyone interested in studying the ghost story, Victorian literature, or these specific authors. It is a pity, yet again, that the price of this volume and others I have examined in this series makes the audience for its insights narrower than it should be, but consultation with a university library by those unable to afford the book will prove worth the time and effort. You will not agree with everything Dr. Lehmann Imfield writes, but I guarantee that she will make you reexamine any position you take on these works from a different angle. Further volumes directing the same level of scrutiny to other authors would be most welcome!

The Weird and Eerie in Finest Form

Daniel Pietersen

JEFFREY THOMAS. *Haunted Worlds.* New York: Hippocampus Press, 2017. 247 pp. $20. tpb. ISBN: 978-1-61498-197-8.

In his book *The Weird and the Eerie* British author Mark Fisher sought to clarify these oft-used but poorly defined terms. The "weird," he states, is characterized by the presence of something that should not, could not, be present. It is an unbalanced state where something has "irrupted," has "pushed-through," into our world from a qualitatively different Elsewhere; it requires a suspension, even a fracture, of natural laws. The sense of the "eerie," on the other hand, occurs when something of our world should be present but is not (or, conversely, when something is present but should not be). A figure that appears silently in the corner of a locked room or a sound that whispers from nowhere: both of these are eerie; they break no laws in themselves, but causality appears to have been fractured to make them occur.

In *Haunted Worlds* Jeffrey Thomas blends these two states almost perfectly, the subtly interlinked tales that make up the collection pervaded with the two forms of this sensory and emotional dislocation.

This interlinked quality is worth addressing before we delve into the stories themselves. Many collections of short stories are simply that—a bundle of tales that sit together but do not speak to one another. There is nothing wrong with this approach, and it is certainly preferable to those collections where the stories seem to be self-aware that they are linked to one another and snigger knowingly, but stories live in a world and should interact with it. Thomas's approach, whether it is consciously undertaken or not, is to seed his stories with similarities that might, but equally might not, place them in the same world. Characters in different stories work in similar jobs, in similar places; insectile pursuers creep from tale to tale; cervine sentinels lurk in woods and at the roadside; narrators stagger between the dead spaces of closing-time malls and vampire worlds; the curious symbols of demon-gods appear in rural America, everyone has lost something, or is destined soon to lose it. This adds a verisimilitude to the individual stories that, perversely, throws the weirder elements into starker relief. We feel that if Lambert, the moribund narrator of the collection's opening tale, "Feeding Oblivion," were told of the centipedes that threaten the inmates of the nursing home, then he would nod almost imperceptibly, recognizing a shared peril. More harrowingly, what he could perhaps have dismissed as his own private delusion would coalesce into a shared experience, a reality.

If a problem shared is a problem halved, then a horror shared is a horror multiplied.

Haunted Worlds itself is divided into two parts, "Our World" and "Other Worlds." The stories that take place in Our World deal very often with the absence that Fisher identifies as a characteristic of the eerie; in "Spider Gates," a young girl disappears, perhaps murdered or perhaps through suicide. Perhaps neither. The story features one of my favorite lines in the entire book, "sadness can make people appear poetic or wistful, when in reality what they're feeling is pain," and has a sadness itself that elevates it beyond what could easily be a King pastiche of childhood trauma. It is only later in the book, in a story about a different place and time, that we understand the significance of the "wheel-like designs" in the eponymous Spider Gates. What started as eerie, pertaining to an absence, now becomes weird, pertaining to an impossibility. Our understanding of the narrative shifts and, as when any assumption is undermined, we feel an abyss yawn beneath us.

In "The Toll," a slight tale that Thomas himself links back to the vignettes of *The Outer Limits,* what starts as a what-if story of alien intercession and impossible choices becomes ever weirder if we connect the "oddly bent forelimbs" and "deer's snout" of the alien with the "deer-like" creature that haunts the narrator of "The Left-Hand Path," its legs "folded up tightly or telescoped somehow." Do these creatures infest our world, selecting the lost and confused for their self-avowed "experimentation"? Are they linked to the albino deer that hides in the woods around the cemetery of Spider Gates?

The collection's central story, "The Green Hands," is pivotal to the whole work in a number of senses. We find another character, Zetter, who is lost and bewildered, pursued by implacable forces and tormented by the absence of his wife. Again we see the eerie, the wife's absence, being enforced by the weird, the inexplicable powers that caused her absence, but the narrative plays out in a very similar manner to the pursuit-dreams that many of us suffer from and which are manifested in the now-common trope of the zombie horde; Thomas even has Zetter's pursuers slap their palms ineffectually on windows, scratching malevolently at cellar doors. Yet, like a dagger in the back, Thomas pierces through his own narrative just as it comes to what would elsewhere be a satis-fying conclusion. The narrative *itself* becomes weird, irrupts into a different mode of being that is unhinged from what has gone before just as we come to realize that Zetter's self-deluded aware-ness has become unhinged from reality. The reader is wrong-footed in a fashion that, rather than being annoying, brings a thrill of novelty. Interestingly, and equally pleasingly, Thomas escalates the dreamlike elements of the tale until, like all dreams, there is only one place left to go: back to the mundane.

This break between the two sections of "The Green Hands" is also the break between the "Our World" stories and those of "Other Worlds." For me, the remaining stories are less effective than those that have gone before. This is not to say that they are worse; in many cases they are more accomplished tales, with greater depth and characterisation; but they are less satisfying. "Good Will toward Men." for example, has some excellent imagery but comes across too obviously as a polemic against religious hypocrisy and ill-thought-out do-goodery. Equally, the two stories set in Thomas's Punktown milieu, "Drawing No. 8" and "Redemption Express," are well crafted but feel overlong after the brevity of those set in Our World. Their consistency and realism fail to shock as the fractured narrative of "The Green Hands" does.

For me, the Our World stories are the most effective because they rely on the corruption of experiences we have all had, if to a lesser degree than what is presented in the narratives. We have all felt that shock of the eerie as we glimpse something in a place it should not be, fear for something not in a place it should be; a malformed figure that resolves on closer inspection into a clump of rain-dampened stones or the sudden nighttime fear that a loved one has disappeared, only to have them emerge from the bathroom, themselves worried by your worry. We smile to ourselves, laugh at our credulity, and make a note to tell our friends what happened. "You won't believe what happened," we chuckle.

What, though, if they truly could not believe? What if the eerie moves to the truly weird? What if the loved one never reappears, vanished as if into nothing? What if that transition from resolvable to irresolvable could happen in an eyeblink, as quickly as turning a page?

This is an excellent collection from an innovative and bold writer. There is little in the way of false hyperbole or lexical grandstanding, as there often can be in weird fiction, which only increases the dream-state realist/surrealist contrast when it arrives. It is a collection that makes me want to write, which is the highest praise I can offer.

Panels of People Screaming:
An Interview with Sarah Horrocks

Nathan Chazan

Sarah Horrocks is an artist on the verge of a major breakthrough. A rising star in small-press and independent comics, Horrocks has become a familiar name on the comics Internet. Her illustrations are sharp, scary, stylish, and intense. They are horror comics, melodramas, and most of all cool comics, memorable for their visual and emotional intensity.

Horrocks is also known for her criticism, appearing on her personal Tumblr as well as in prominent publications such as The Comics Journal. Her criticism stands out for its eloquent interpretations of the sublime power of a striking illustration. Horrocks has also written extensively about horror movies (most recently in a series of backup essays in the Image comic *Winnebago Graveyard*), serious and thoughtful examinations of the aesthetics of brutality on film. In her 2014–17 podcast "Trash Twins," Horrocks and fellow cartoonist Katie Skelly would "dig through the trash they love," sharing enthusiasm for movies and comics that live in that muddy space between art and pulp. Her own stories exist in that same space of storytelling which worms its way into the reader's mind and stays there.

Horrocks's longest work to date is *The Leopard,* a love letter to giallo (Italian crime and mystery) films and an explosion of the genre. A self-published serialization of five chapters (counting a prologue) first published digitally on her Gumroad website from 2015 to 2017, *The Leopard* is the story of a family of bohemians who visit their dying mother on a private island straight out of a '70s Mario Bava movie. The family members resent their mother for her cruelty as a parent and take out their frustrations on Ophele, their trans sister, who endures abuse both verbal and physical. However, the mother's estate is valuable, and things get bloody fast, as potential heirs are picked off until only one is left standing. *The Leopard* is an idiosyncratic and emotionally charged resurrection of giallo, exploring a type of fear never directly

named in a giallo film—transphobia. Horrocks is now beginning a new series called *Goro,* an ambitious work that she intends to serialize monthly. This past summer, I had the chance to talk to Horrocks via email about melodrama, aesthetics, horror, violence, dysphoria, and how these all came together in *The Leopard*.

NC: I really appreciate the intensity of your images, not only in terms of their violence but in the weight of inkwork, the overwhelming primary colors, the experimental layouts . . . You create pages that are immediately appealing but take time to process. What do you tend to think about when you're creating these compositions?

SH: It's more emotional than anything. I've always admired artists like [Egon] Schiele and [Bill] Sienkiewicz who could communicate emotion just in their line, but I want even more. So how I draw, how I color, and how I do my layouts . . . I'm very focused on the emotion. It's not really important to me to have consistency of color or figure from panel to panel to page—I more want those things to both communicate the right-there-and-then of the page and be working in concert with the rest of the book. So when I color, I usually like to do it all at once after the book is drawn, and I'll lay all the pages out and just kind of emotionally flip through the colors and carve out certain suites of colors, and then connect them to each other. But it's all just kind of by feel. I think a lot of people have developed systems which makes them more efficient probably, but for me, I know it when I see it, and there's not always a rule that fits or makes sense for doing a particular panel a particular way. I just kind of have it in my head, and then try my best to do the least fucked up version of what's in my head.

NC: What sort of planning goes into your stories? Are they intricately conceived or do you figure things out as you go along?

SH: Yeah, I have to script in advance so I know what the beats are, and because of the way I organize my life, it's better for me to sit down each day and have the script already figured out and just work off of it. Usually I kind of feel like the drawing phase is another rewriting chance, so I will tweak things as I'm drawing them—either the dialogue, or if I'm drawing a page and it makes sense for it to be two pages, or to condense two pages into one because one page is too empty—then I do that kind of thing. I have the whole thing mapped out in outline form as well, but I generally will only write about 30 to 60 pages ahead of when I'm drawing, because otherwise, I think it can get quite stale. I want the story to feel fluid up until the last page I draw, and then it locks into place and I'm done. I've completely written out a long script in the past, and those comics are ones I've never ended up doing. And usually I just end up kind of cannibalizing those kinds of things for other things. It just doesn't work for me to have everything done. Plus if I do it that way then I just am drawing for months on end, and I like to write, so it allows me to kind of draw for a month, write for two weeks, draw for a month, write for two weeks. Which feels more balanced.

NC: You've described [ED: http://bit.ly/2x2ZdYj] *The Leopard* as a "transphobic revenge giallo." What was your first encounter with giallo and Italian horror?

SH: Hmm . . . probably *Suspiria* in terms of Italian horror. Not sure what my first giallo was. I was very late to horror because I was a really frightened kid growing up. Very terrified of aliens, death, and Satan. As I got older and more numb, the things that still affected me are the things that I was drawn the most toward, so that's when I started watching horror, more as an adult. Now I love all the things that used to terrify me. *The Bird with the Crystal Plumage* was probably my first proper giallo, though I think *Leopard* is more indebted to Bava and Fulci than Argento. I also watched the OG *Texas Chainsaw Massacre* on loop for 48 hours to get into the mood for the last volume of *Leopard*. It's not a giallo, but that chase scene is my all-time favorite.

NC: Were there any viewing experiences that were particularly seminal in creating *The Leopard*?

SH: *5 Dolls for an August Moon* and *Bay of Blood*. Also Bergman's *Cries and Whispers*. Oh, also *Cat People,* especially the Paul Schrader remake. [My comic] is actually called *The Leopard* after Val Lewton's *The Leopard Man*, which I've never seen, but in my head I imagined [*The Leopard*] as *Cat People* but with a leopard.

And since I know it's not really that, I'm not ever going to see it. But that's where the title came from. Not the Visconti movie.

NC: *The Leopard* is about a wealthy family murdering each other to get an inheritance, a very Mario Bava plot that also allows you to explore a lot of melodramatic situations and extravagant fashion. Another recent comic of yours, *Leviathan,* tackles old Hollywood with a very explicit rendition of an aging starlet's fall from grace. What appeals to you about melodrama?

SH: I feel like the comic medium is great at melodrama because melodrama is this very direct, kinda trashy exploration of human relationships, and it's a lot of heightened emotions, so lots of panels of people screaming or crying, and saying that one awful thing to each other. Plus it's not so big in comics right now. At least in the west. A lot of people want to make these kind of long drawn out airy sandbox comics where people don't have a lot of intense personal relationships, romantically or otherwise. I love the intensity of a love triangle, or unrequited love. Just people affecting one another in ways that aren't subtle. With comics I feel like it's better to scream it. So melodrama is the perfect vehicle for this. I think too because when you read comics, there's the comic on the page and the comic in your head, these broad strokes create the space for the reader to fill in with themselves and become more emotionally invested in the work. So I try for that. My next book *Goro* is very much like soap opera, telenovela. Like *Dynasty*. Almodovar. Maria La Del Barrio. Awful people being awful and glamorous.

NC: You wrote an essay [ED: http://bit.ly/2gv2eG0] last year where you referred to the "defiance" of transkiller narratives. Are you trying to reclaim transphobia in horror or is there something more idiosyncratic at play?

SH: I don't know if I'm trying to reclaim it or not, but I am definitely interested in how trans women in particular are portrayed in genre works. And then why. I think with *The Leopard* I wanted to make it so that instead of being freaked out by the trans character, you were freaked out by the people around her and how they treated her, which very much tilts what goes on in the book from being a straight up monster movie comic, to being about a comeback on hate. Or like . . . the hate that hate made, I guess. Like maybe a lot of cis people hate or fear me for being trans, but that lens can work both ways, buddies. Basically.

NC: Let's talk about gore. *The Leopard* is an extremely violent comic, and the depiction of that violence is very striking. The third chapter in particular has these great images of skeletons, spines, and internal organs being forcibly torn out of cleaved bodies, as though the insides are rebelling against the skin that contains them. What do these images mean to you?

SH: Most days there's some point where I fantasize about pulling all my skin off. Or bashing my bones into all these fragments. Or my bones coming out of my body like knives. So gore for me is very therapeutic, and I like to look at fake, really over the top expressionistic gore. It's hard for me to look at [real blood], like when I was a kid I used to pass out at needles, and like trips to the hospital. Even now I don't watch them draw my blood and I can't watch medical things. But I feel like seeing an image of entrails on Tumblr or something, it's kind of soothing to my body dysmorphia. Every day in my body is basically about not fitting within spaces, and this constant clawing at what my body is and what it should be and then somewhere in there is what I want it to be. It's just a soup that sits in my stomach and I have no way to get it out. So drawing these kinds of things is me trying to get it out. Hopefully that's not a completely disturbing way of explaining things. I wish I could have drawn the gore even worse. Like Shintaro Kago or [Hiroaki] Samura's *Brute Love* level. Or Suehiro Maruo licking eyeball stuff. But not yet. Someday maybe!

NC: In *The Plague,* the backup story in *The Leopard Vol. 0,* your characters have a conversation about Lucio Fulci movies and the protagonist says she wants "to see a movie where someone bleeds in bubbles." Your work seems to be informed by a similarly perverse desire for fantastic bloodshed. What do you think makes us want to see these things?

SH: I think it's repression. The desire for that which is inside of us to be outside of us. Like have you ever smelled something that's died? Or seen a rat out of the corner of your eye? Even though intellectually you understand these are just things in the world, and they aren't really a threat to you—you still kind of retch or have a very visceral reaction. How many things can do that to you in your life? Beauty does that too. You see something beautiful, and you gasp for air. It's Medusa or that notion that if you see god's face you go insane—it's linked to the idea that in order to live you have to maintain desire, so our ideas of beauty can never totally satiate desire otherwise we die. Death is the only true beauty, because you cease living after experiencing it. Everything else is death's shadow. We live in that shadow. So these things that move us, they are linked to our desire to live within the framework of our journey towards death. Gore and horror are the truest, easiest form of beauty to explore, because the other kind of beauty has been so profaned and distorted by capitalism—all that's really left that we can see is fear, death, mortality, blood. These are the things which reliably stop us in our tracks the most—the things that you see and you feel it in your whole body.

NC: There are a lot of references to mothers in *The Leopard*—the family's disdain for their dying matriarch, the grotesque birth imagery, the final words of the epilogue. Would you say a little about this theme?

SH: I think it's been a theme in all my work so far. And my next comic *Goro* also has this theme. I think it is linked to a few different things. One is that motherhood and your relation to it is kind of this looming shadow of being a woman. Even as a trans woman, I'm somewhat defined by the inability to have children, it's really not even on the table for me—and not that I want any, but I think it's linked to an anxiety of not being woman enough. The other aspect of it that crops up in my work is that of the interior double who in being brought to the surface causes an apocalypse. This is a much larger aspect of almost every comic I've done, I think. It's not something I consciously set out to do, but I end up in that spot in my stories almost every time. And I think that's just basically that I lived my life for like my childhood and teens carrying this perception of myself, and when I brought it from the inside to the outside, it turned my world upside down,

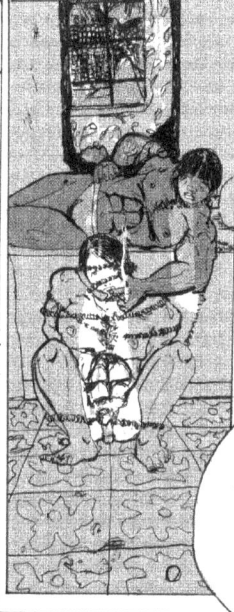

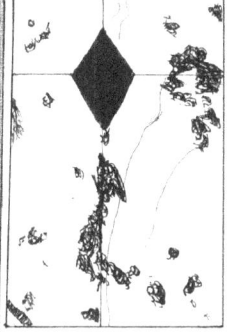

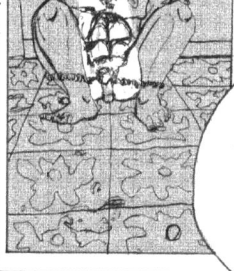

and I mostly live in the wasteland of who I am. What I wanted to try with *Leopard* was to create a relationship between this trans woman and this other woman where the apocalypse of coming out turned the sort of straight cisgender world upside down— but for the trans woman she's able to get what she wants, which going back to the first theme ends up being a demon baby to have with her lover. So I think it was both an attack on cis het norm stuff, and like this desire to depict a queer trans family coming out of the ashes of that. But that even in that context, the child is still kind of that dark double. Sort of the next generation of trouble. That would be my guess anyways. Even *Bruise,* which is a comic I made expressly as the exact opposite of anything I would want to make (dudes action car cyberpunk comic), still has these themes, because the two men combine with their car and the city to transform the city into their apocalyptic sexual creation. Ha. I pretty much have to make horror with these sorts of running themes in my work.

NC: *The Leopard* is your longest sustained narrative to date. Has your work changed in the process?

SH: I'm a lot better at drawing. I kind of leveled up I think between vol. 3 and 4 but still had to stay in the sort of *Leopard* style. But I think anyone who has seen my newer work, you can see I had a style shift coming out of this. I think I learned a lot about what worked for me on the page, and what didn't. When I first started *Leopard* I thought it was going to be more textured, with more sort of marks on the page—but in the end, it's just about forms and lines. I also kind of got sick of color because of *Leopard*. I might feel differently in a year, but right now I'm pretty over color. I really like black and white that's very expressionistic, and has different tones in it. It's nice to do those things and not have to also think about the palette. There's just not many colors I like right now.

NC: In addition to your own comics, you're well known online for your writing about comics and horror movies. When I read your comics, it's hard for me not to think at times of your critical voice as well. How much do you want your audience to think about your influences?

SH: I would say try not to. I think a lot of times, even though I clearly delineate my influences—just follow me on Twitter or Instagram and you can see exactly where my aesthetic comes out of—but in spite of that people guess a lot, and usually it's just based on what they know in their own lives—so what they are really communicating is a shorthand for what they're seeing, but trying to see things through other things obscures them. Right now I'm really wrestling with my Kyoko Okazaki influence and trying to figure out how to communicate where her work hits me, with my own lines, so it like is my thing, not her thing.

So I dunno. I don't know if me being a critic as well helps or hurts my work, because I'm sure if I just put the work out on its own without having anything else to say to people about comics in general, it would look like it was from outer space, and might hit harder. But I care so much about comics—and art in general—that it's hard for me to bite my tongue. I have thoughts about what I like and why, and me even making comics comes from a place of not seeing anything even remotely representing how I see. Everything I read, I'm like "oh man, I wish it was this instead" or "I wish they had done this thing here but really amped it up"—that shit makes me really restless, and so I have to do my thing. With criticism it's the same thing. People don't talk about the books I like, and if they do, they do it in a way I hate—so I just do it myself. Plus criticism helps me creatively to figure out more clearly my own POV.

NC: You're working on a new comic right now called *Goro,* which will probably be available in some form by the time this interview is published. Can you say a little about what we can expect from this work?

SH: It's a black and white comic that I'm going to release monthly in print starting in probably September. I'm almost done with the first volume which is 24 pages. I'm trying to plan it right so I have enough of it in stock before I start putting it out. So it will be around 16–24 pages per volume. Ten volumes. It will come out like two months in print, and then every third month there will be a digital collection for the previous two months. So ten print volumes. Five digital volumes.

Dead Reckonings

It's basically a soap opera. This Colombian assassin comes to America to kill an evil wealthy matriarch is basically how I've been synopsizing it to the Internet. But it's more like *Dynasty* or *Dallas* than like . . . *The Killer*. I think people are going to like it. My art is finally to that point where I see other comics, and a lot of the time I'm like "yeah it's good, but not as good as miiiiine." So we'll see. I would say it's visually most similar to *Goatlord* but much more developed.

Vibrant and Vivid: NecronomiCon 2017

Elena Tchougounova-Paulson

It has been a few weeks since I came back from Providence to Cambridge, but my memories about the trip are still as vibrant and vivid as if everything happened only yesterday. For me it means a lot, and first and foremost, the actual journey was an absolutely unforgettable life experience.

The main event of NecronomiCon, in my opinion as an academic, was the Armitage Symposium and all its panels: finally, I met people who were involved in the different fields of Lovecraftiana (including cultural, Gothic, and neo-Gothic American/Western European studies) after many years; also my colleagues, literary and textual scholars and publishers, who edited Lovecraft's fiction, essays, and enormous correspondence with a variety of authors.

My first essential part in the convention was participation at the panel "Women in the Lovecraft Circle." I have talked to people who had met some of Lovecraft's friends and acquaintances, and this was beyond incredible; we have also discussed the writings of Lovecraft's female correspondents (including his wife, Sonia Greene, whose memoirs are a significant textual source for Lovecraft researchers) and their engagement with *Weird Tales*. As a result of this, I purchased a unique edition of the correspondence between Lovecraft and Zealia Bishop, *The Spirit of Revision*. That was prepared by one of the participants at the panel, Sean Branney, who is a well-known actor and also a director and writer in the H. P. Lovecraft Historical Society. I highly appreciate the kind support of my colleagues, whom I first met at this panel, Faye Ringel and Scott Connors, who made the whole discussion truly fascinating.

My own international panel, "Emanations of Abominations: Lovecraft Around the Globe," was the turning point of my Providence trip: I was overwhelmed. I delivered a talk, "Alexander Blok and H. P. Lovecraft: On the Mythopoetics of the Supernatural," the first essay that compares two literary figures, H. P. Lovecraft and the Russian poet-Symbolist from the same era, Alexander Blok. To be fair, I didn't expect considerable feedback afterwards: usually I make a brief introduction for the English-speaking audience about Blok and his role in Russian fin-de-siècle (sadly, although he is widely known among Slavic scholars, he is not at all famous in the Western academic milieu), but I did not have time for any remarks of that sort. To my great surprise, participants began asking me about Blok with full professional awareness— about him taking part in World War I, writing the poem "The Twelve," etc. That was incredible! And, of course, the whole discussion about the conceivable parallels between Blok and Lovecraft looked entirely coherent. Many thanks to the chair of the panel, Fred S. Lubnow, for his kind assistance, as well as to all my colleagues and participants.

In conclusion, I just want to add that Providence with its marvelous and very special Zeitgeist is now one of my favorite cities, alongside Cambridge and St. Petersburg, and I do hope to return there as soon as possible.

Nevertheless, She Persisted

Bev Vincent

STEPHEN KING and OWEN KING. *Sleeping Beauties*. New York: Scribner, 2017. 702 pp. $32.50 hc. ISBN: 978-1-5011-6340-1.

In Ernest Jones's *Sigmund Freud: Life and Work,* Freud offered the following observation: "The great question that has never been answered, and which I have not yet been able to answer, despite my thirty years of research into the feminine soul, is 'What does a woman want?'"

A pivotal character in *Sleeping Beauties*, the collaborative novel between Stephen King and his younger son Owen, quotes this passage and offers her answer: "I think most women, if you asked them, if they were truly honest, what they would say is, they want a nap."

A nap they shall have. A mysterious epidemic sweeps the globe in a single day. Any woman already asleep remains asleep. Additionally, the women become encased in gauzy cocoons. Woe betide him who disrupts a cocoon: an awakened woman is ferocious, lashing out with superhuman force at anyone except pre-adolescent children.

Owen King brought the idea of a world where all the women go to sleep to his father just before America experienced a resurgence in awareness of women's rights—before the Million Woman March, for example, or the popular adaptation of *A Handmaid's Tale*—so the book's exploration of pervasive misogyny is timely. The elder King immediately thought of all the possible repercussions of the scenario, and the two decided to write the story together.

Women who are still awake are fine so long as they stay that way. Once they succumb to sleep, they join their sisters in preternatural slumber—and no one knows if they will ever reawaken. This creates one of the novel's conflicts: the struggle by women to remain awake. The world record is eleven days, but even a couple of days without sleep causes slowed reflexes, short-term memory problems, irritability, impaired judgment, and hallucinations.

Although the epidemic spans the globe, *Sleeping Beauties* is set in Dooling County, West Virginia, where the main employer is a women's prison. The sheriff is female, as is the prison warden. Because Dooling is in the Eastern time zone, most of the women there were awake at the onset of the affliction, dubbed "Aurora" after the character from Disney's *Sleeping Beauty*. They start the day with a "full tank" of sleep and make use of every artificial means available to fend off sleep. Gradually, though, their numbers dwindle. Many, believing the outcome inevitable, surrender to sleep.

Women have been restraining men from their baser instincts throughout history. What will society become without their moderating influence? Will there be an upsurge in senseless violence? If the men of the world went to sleep, civilization could survive, thanks to a robust supply of frozen sperm. Even if new male offspring went to sleep, civilization might persist long enough to outlast whatever is causing this situation. Without women, though, the world is doomed. Procreation comes to a screeching halt. In less than a century, humanity will end, unless a solution is found.

Dooling is ground zero for the affliction, even though it started on the other side of the globe. A mysterious and beautiful woman who calls herself Evie Black shows up at the edge of town, wreaks sufficient carnage on a meth lab to attract the attention of the police, and does herself physical harm to get sent to the prison for psychiatric evaluation. She is no ordinary woman . . . perhaps not human at all. She heals rapidly and can summon animals to do her bidding. Did she cause this situation or is she taking advantage of it? Is she a female Randall Flagg, creating chaos, or a Gaia figure, an avatar of Nature attempting to restore balance to an off-kilter world?

Though Evie needs no man to protect her, she surrenders herself to the care of Clint Norcross, the prison psychologist. As men go, he is pretty liberal and feminist, but he is far from perfect. He steadfastly refuses to discuss his troubled childhood with his wife—the sheriff—which has led to a recent breakdown in communications between them. He also has a history of making unilateral decisions that are bones of contention his wife gnaws on regularly: the backyard pool he gave her as an anniversary gift she did not want, for example, and his impulsive decision to quit private practice—a job she relocated to facilitate—to work at the prison.

As the situation in town worsens, word gets out that a woman at the prison can go to sleep and wake up again. Clint and the skeleton crew remaining at the prison are tasked with keeping Evie safe from the angry mob in town that insists she be turned over to them so that tests can be done and a cure possibly discovered. Clint is level-headed and rational, yet he is prone to making decisions for others. Is he right to keep Evie from the townfolk? Readers might find themselves wondering which side they would align themselves with if placed in a similar situation.

There is an unassailable logic to examining the one person

who appears to be immune to a disease, and there is also the open question of whether destroying a "Typhoid Mary" in the hopes of saving humanity is justifiable. There is nothing particularly evil about the people who lobby for Evie's release into their custody: these are mostly good men who come from a society where violence is always an option when it comes to solving a problem. Still, there are those who believe that women deserve this curse because they have deigned to pull even with their male counterparts in less than a century. In some ways, perhaps, they are pulling ahead, and this will not stand. Rumors and fake news spread over the Internet, giving some men the excuse they need to take drastic action toward their sleeping companions.

The de facto leader of the opposition is Frank Geary, a man with anger management issues. He is separated from his wife and daughter because of his violent outbursts. He believes he acts in their best interests, but acknowledges that a "Bad Frank" breaks free from time to time. He is too unwilling to let small stuff go to qualify for the Dooling Police Department, so he works as the town's animal control officer. Despite his temper, he tries to work within the system to gain access to Evie before resorting to violence. He is of a type that has appeared in other Stephen King novels: a man who manipulates weaker men into doing his bidding, preferring to operate from the sidelines. Big Jim Rennie from *Under the Dome,* for example, or Flagg in *The Eyes of the Dragon*. The patsy here is the alcoholic deputy who takes over after Sheriff Norcross succumbs to sleep.

Sleeping Beauties has an enormous cast. The dramatis personae at the front of the book runs for four pages and lists more than seventy characters (and a fox). The first half of this 700-page novel details the first twenty-four hours after the outbreak. The Kings have a lot of pieces on their chessboard to establish, but it would be impossible to care about what happens in the second half of the novel if readers were not already invested in these characters. That is not to say the first 350 pages are without incident: a lot happens, certainly, but it is mostly to get things and people into position for "the stand" that is the business of the rest of the novel.

The book is dedicated to the memory of Sandra Bland, who was pulled over for a traffic violation and died in jail. A significant amount of the action takes place inside the prison. Most of the women have been incarcerated for non-violent offenses, although a few are behind bars for manslaughter or murder. Many are in prison because of trouble with a man.

The question of what the world would look like if it had been the men who went to sleep has been raised recently, with news of an all-female remake of William Golding's *Lord of the Flies*. The announcement was met with derision, along with a number of comedic renderings of what that adaptation would look like. The Kings explore this concept via an alternate reality called "Our Place," where the women from Dooling find themselves after falling asleep, a reproduction of Dooling, although an untold number of years have passed and much has crumbled and decayed. Time moves differently here. There is little by way of technology remaining, but it is a real place to them. In a scenario akin to the Boulder Free Committee sections of *The Stand,* they reestablish society, rebuilding some of the things that have been lost. It is a testosterone-lite environment, which gives the Kings a chance to examine the other side of the coin.

The Kings passed the story back and forth "like tennis, like [*sic*] the book is the ball," they said in an interview. Subsequently they rewrote each other's work, arriving at a seamless third voice unlike either writer's. This is a major achievement, given the dramatic difference between their respective styles. Although the book is massive, it never drags. Even minor characters are given due attention, which is important because one never knows when someone will step up to the plate at a pivotal moment. Because of its timely and relevant social commentary, this book will likely generate a lot of discussion. The battle of the sexes is alive and well in 2017.

It is somewhat ironic that the word "woke" has become synonymous with burgeoning social awareness—a woke male is attuned to the plight of contemporary women—given that the novel is about a sleeping sickness. Of course, there may be concerns about two white males shining a spotlight on problems and issues faced by women from every culture on a daily basis. However, while *Sleeping Beauties* does highlight these issues, it is also a damning indictment of the contemporary male. Even the good ones do not get off lightly. As one observer says in the midst of a barroom melee: women are sane, but men are mad.

Thinking Visually: Comments on Comics

Alex Houstoun

GOU TANABE. *H. P. Lovecraft's The Hound and Other Stories*. Translated by Zack Davisson. Milwaukie, OR: Dark Horse, 2017. 184 pp. $12.99 tpb. ISBN: 978-1-50670-312-1.

"Man is so used to thinking visually," Lovecraft writes in "The Nameless City," and it is this default mode of thinking that has often let me feeling frustrated when reading graphic adaptations of Lovecraft's stories. Lovecraft uses very intentional language in his work to describe entities that cannot be readily visualized or, as is so often elaborated by his characters, whose physical presences represent a shattering of humanity's known understanding of the world. While it is possible to convey this effect in a written story—granted, this requires very precise work on the part of the author (and Lovecraft has his share of stories that fail on execution)—it tends to fall flat in comics, given the visual nature of the medium. The artist is presented with the seemingly paradoxical task of illustrating something that is supposed to be a reality-bending entity that cannot be fully comprehended by the human brain. As such, artists of adaptations have to choose between acknowledging the inherent shortcoming of the medium and perhaps taking a campier route—I am thinking in particular of Richard Corben's *Haunt of Horror: Lovecraft* series for MAX and the various stories done in *Creepy* over the years—or missing the mark entirely and presenting the reader with a reductive version of Cthulhu and all its tentacle-clichéd glory.

Enter Gou Tanabe who has, for the past ten years, been publishing his adaptations of Lovecraft stories in Japan and now has a collection of three of those stories available in the U.S. courtesy of Dark Horse—the titular tale along with adaptations of "The Temple" and "The Nameless City." While it may be a bit overblown to render judgment on a decade's worth of work on a slim collection such as this, I must say that Tanabe's adaptations are the some of the best I have ever encountered.

So what makes Tanabe the exception to my prior lamentations? A large part of the success is due to the stories he has adapted. These stories are much more about atmosphere and mood than they are about a physical, otherworldly horror revealed in a climax. Tanabe proves himself an expert at developing tension across panels. In particular, he uses black, uses it liberally, and uses it in such a way that makes one feel as though his characters are on the verge of being swallowed by an unknown darkness. This works textually as well visually: the eye is drawn from black space to black space, trapped with the characters in a submarine or an underground ancient ruin.

Tanabe embraces the fact that he is working in a visual medium and relies on minimal words when he can. This leads to pages of silence in which the reader is left to appreciate Tanabe's truly excellent line work. While there is minimal variety in his living characters, Tanabe displays a great talent for intricate detail and setting—the statues and ruins in "The Temple" are truly incredible, as is a full-page spread from "The Nameless City" that I refuse to spoil in any manner. This attention to detail, allowing the setting to be discovered and digested by the reader, does so much more than Lovecraft's words could do in a visual medium. Instead of relying on language to convey the stories' horrors, Tanabe has subtly presented them, letting the reader absorb them all in their own time.

My prior claim that these three stories are ones that rely on tension and mood rather than physical horrors is admittedly untrue, both given the source material and what Tanabe does in his adaptations. There is a beast in "The Hound," and we see evidence of its physical prowess as well as suggestions as to what it may actually be. There are hints and panels that suggest what sort of creatures inhabit the nameless city. However, in both cases Tanabe obscures as much as he shows: the creatures are hidden in shadows or distorted; we are left with the bit he provides, allowing our imaginations and the suggestions of the story fill in the rest. This blank space or gap has always been what draws me to Lovecraft's work, and I am grateful that Tanabe seems to reflect a similar sort of worldview vis-à-vis Lovecraft: it is not for him to render and define what may horrify and terrorize each reader.

I was extremely familiar with these stories prior to reading this collection, and yet I still found myself dreading their endings—I feared what Tanabe was capable of and how it might scare me in a way that reading Lovecraft for the first time did. The collection ends with a note stating that "Dark Horse hopes to publish further volumes of Tanabe's Lovecraft adaptations in the future." I can only hope that future is not too far off.

Revisiting the Dreamlands

Darrell Schweitzer

KIJ JOHNSON. *The Dream-Quest of Vellitt Boe*. New York: Tor.com, 2016. 169 pp. $14.99 tpb. ISBN 978-0-7653-9141-4.

Everybody's doing Lovecraft these days, from N. K. Jemison to Victor LaValle to Matt Ruff. The thing to keep in mind when reading some later writer's re-imaginings of Lovecraft's material or expansions on his themes is that like any great writer, Lovecraft belongs to the world now. His work is a part of the culture, the same as Shakespeare's or Poe's or Bram Stoker's *Dracula*. Anybody can play. There are no rules. No group can claim to "own" Lovecraft anymore, and certainly there is no orthodoxy to defend. It is therefore useless to critique such a work on the basis that it is "not Lovecraftian" or that "Lovecraft wouldn't have done it this way." No, he wouldn't. He didn't. Somebody else did. Ideally, the only valid criterion is whether or not the work is successful on its own terms.

That being said, I have to confess that I did not find *The Dream-Quest of Vellitt Boe* very effective. This is not the first visit to the Dreamlands, the setting of *The Dream-Quest of Unknown Kadath,* by another writer. Brian Lumley set a whole series of novels there in the 1980s. But what I notice about the place, as reported by Kij Johnson, is that it has become almost mundane. All the wonder has been leached out. There is a women's college in Ulthar now, and Ulthar sounds about as exotic, as a college town, as Newark, Delaware. Even when the heroine begins to travel, the landscapes are very ordinary, for the most part. Farms. Country roads. Inns. There is still a zoog forest, and capricious gods may lurk behind it all, but the Dreamlands are just another country. In a change of perspective from Lovecraft, it is seen from the point of view of the natives, no longer a mystical realm only reachable by dreamers in exalted states, but home. The "waking world" is something most natives have never seen and can scarcely imagine.

The title character is a fifty-five-year-old professor at the women's college. A crisis arises when one of her students has eloped with a dreamer from the waking world. Why precisely this is a crisis, beyond the level of social scandal, we do not learn until we are well along into the story. It seems the girl is the granddaughter of a god, who might just wipe Ulthar off the map if sufficiently displeased. Vellitt Boe, who was a seasoned traveler in her youth, is convinced she is the only one who can convince the girl to come back. So off she goes, but, title to the contrary, this is not a dream-quest at all, merely a quest, a matter of long hikes and ship voyages and pauses to question people who might have seen the fleeing lovers.

There's not much tension. The narrative falls into a common trap of second- or third-hand Dunsanianism (something Ursula K. Le Guin warned us against years ago in "From Elfland to Poughkeepsie"), which is that once the author has given one more fabulous city an exotic name, made a few observations about the architecture or materials (marble, chalcedony, onyx, or whatever), there is all too often nothing actually there.

Arguably very little happens until the shantak attack on page 116. Adventures among ghouls, ghasts, and gugs follow for a few pages. Vellitt then makes her way into the waking world, emerges in Wisconsin, finds the missing girl (whose lover dumped her a while ago), and quickly persuades her to go back into Dreamland to set things right. She herself, for a variety of reasons, cannot return, and seems set up for sequels, as if her Dreamland existence is just a backstory for something more interesting to come.

Indeed, the whole book seems to be a set-up for something better. In the last few pages Johnson does begin to explore the relationship between the dream world and the waking world, and the plot finally gets into gear. There are indeed conniving gods behind it all, and a spy is trailing her, and her some of her old friendships from her adventurous youth have come into play, but the structure and pacing are all wrong. The story takes much too long to become more than mildly engaging, and then is over before it has scarcely begun.

Johnson has added some things to the Dreamlands mythos, most notably women. There are none in the original Lovecraft novella, but too be fair, other than Randolph Carter, there are few human characters of any kind. Johnson shows us strong, capable, and willful women native to the Dreamlands. Vellitt Boe was once a lover to Randolph Carter, but found him too self-absorbed, which is a shrewd bit of characterization, because anybody who undertakes a dangerous quest to the ends of the cosmos to gratify his own visionary longings is indeed likely to be caught up in himself. Carter is king in Ilek-Vad these days. Boe and he are still friends, but they are not going back together. Of course in Lovecraft, Randolph Carter was last seen trapped in an alien body, disappearing into de Marigny's clock at the end of "Through the Gates of the Silver Key." How he got from there back into Dreamland in human form is perhaps a tale yet to be told.

I suppose we ultimately can't escape comparing this to Lovecraft. *The Dream-Quest of Vellitt Boe* of course lacks Lovecraft's sonorous prose. This is wise, because most attempts by other writers to imitate Lovecraft style have been disastrous. That she has added to the range of the cast of characters (Nasht the High Priest is gay, by the way) is interesting. But what amounts to a domestication of the Dreamlands is a lot less interesting. What this book needs, other than better pacing, is to be considerably more *weird,* in every sense of the word.

A Reflection: NecronomiCon 2017

Dr. Géza A. G. Reilly

NecronomiCon 2017 came at my wife and me like a freight train, since we did not make the decision to attend until a month before the convention. I had never been to a NecronomiCon, or Providence itself, despite having devoted the past ten years to the scholarly study of weird fiction. Time and finances always seemed to get in the way, and I thus knew of the city and convention only through fiction, criticism, and fandom. The only sour note to our preparation was the sudden self-removal of S. T. Joshi from any of the formal proceedings. Joshi was among the many persons I had long admired and looked forward to meeting; the thought that I would not be able to do so left a hole in my anticipation of the coming milestone. There were still many others I would be able to meet, but I would be lying if I said that I did not feel as though the experience was lessened.

That feeling has only deepened since the convention itself. Many persons, including Joshi, have fallen into trenches that I dearly wish they would emerge from. Out of these deeply dug emplacements, individuals on all sides seem content to hurl invective in the name of the things that should be bringing us all together. What NecronomiCon showed me is that all involved are motivated by the better angels of their natures—the preservation and production of the weird tradition—and yet they have allowed their all-too-human flaws to degrade the very sense of play and imagination that Steven J. Mariconda passionately called for during his opening address.

I ended the weekend at NecronomiCon by visiting Lovecraft's grave with my wife and a friend from many years ago. It was a moving moment for me, to be there, on Lovecraft's birthday, face to face with the inevitable fact of mortality. The days preceding, all the panels and sessions of the symposium I had enjoyed, the people I had met and shared conversation with, the pleasant numbness of wandering the vendor's halls, the walks through Lovecraft's neighborhood, all faded away as the sight of Lovecraft's tombstone eclipsed everything else.

My NecronomiCon 2017 was a whirlwind, the culmination of years of work and decades of interest. I think I could write dozens of pages on the most minute elements of my experience. I likely will be processing the convention mentally for months to come. And yet, now, in retrospect, all I can think of is Lovecraft's grave. Life is short and the grave is deep; Lovecraft was flawed and Lovecraft was admirable. Weird fiction, whatever it was and whatever it is, will leave us in the ground long before it is exhausted.

Let us then not remember NecronomiCon 2017 as the moment of the fracture of our tiny, insignificant, playful community. Let us remember NecronomiCon 2017 as the moment when we almost irrevocably tore ourselves apart from one another—then returned, in dignity and poise, to one another and our shared love of our work.

About the Contributors

Michael J. Abolafia is an editor, writer, archivist with a B.A. in English from Columbia University, and co-editor of *Dead Reckonings*.

Martin Andersson of Sweden teaches Swedish and English. With S. T. Joshi he co-edited Lord Dunsany's *The Ghost in the Corner and Other Stories*.

Jason V Brock is a writer, editor, filmmaker, composer, artist, scholar, and speaker. He has been widely published online, in comic books, magazines, and anthologies.

Ramsey Campbell is an English horror fiction writer, editor and critic who has been writing for well over fifty years. He is frequently cited as one of the leading writers in the field. His website is www.ramseycampbell.com.

Nathan Chazan is from Toronto, Canada. He is an undergraduate classics major at Cornell University. His writing has previously appeared in *Cleaver Magazine* and the *Cornell Daily Sun*.

Jeanne D'Angelo is a painter of illustrations living and working in Philadelphia. You may have seen her work on for Anya Martin's *Grass* (Dim Shores) or her *Unclean Spirits* zine (Seventh Church Ministries) or a variety of collaborations and commissions from writers, bands and other projects. Her work can be found at http://jeannemdangelo.com.

Barry Lee Dejasu is a reviewer for *New York Journal of Books* and a staff writer for the movie website *Cinema Knife Fight*. He has also had nonfiction published in the magazines *Modern Fix* and *Shock Totem* and is a member of New England Horror Writers. He lives in Providence, Rhode Island, with his wife.

Dave Felton's scratchboard illustrations have appeared in books published by Dim Shores, Dunhams Manor Press, and the Lovecraft eZine.

Tony Fonseca is a librarian at Elms College in Massachusetts. He has co-authored three volumes of *Hooked on Horror* (with June Michele Pulliam), as well as *Read On . . . Horror,* and has contributed to *Icons of Horror and the Supernatural* and *Encyclopedia of the Vampire* (both edited by S. T. Joshi), and was a reviewer with *Necrofile*. He has published articles on gender-based reactions to horror and on vampire music, and on Ramsey Campbell, *Dracula's Daughter/Nadja,* and Robert Aickman. His study of Richard Matheson (with June Pulliam) has appeared from Rowman & Littlefield.

Greg Gbur is a professor of physics and optical science at UNCC Charlotte. For more than a decade he has written a blog called Skulls in the Stars (https://skullsinthestars.com) about physics, horror fiction, and curious intersections between them. He has written a number of introductions to classic reprinted horror novels for Valancourt Books.

Stephanie Graves is an instructor at the University of North Alabama and is currently pursuing her Ph.D. in English at Georgia State University. Her research interests include horror, the grotesque, and the Southern Gothic.

Sarah Horrocks makes and writes about comics. She has done cover work for various Image Comics and Boom Studios comics. She has done critical writing about comics for *Fantagraphics, ComicsAlliance, Study Group Magazine,* and *The Comics Journal.* Her newest comic is *Goro* is available at http://mercurialblonde. storenvy.com/.

Alex Houstoun is a co-editor of *Dead Reckonings.*

S. T. Joshi is the author of such critical studies as *The Weird Tale* (1990), *H. P. Lovecraft: The Decline of the West* (1990), and *Unutterable Horror: A History of Supernatural Fiction* (2012). He has prepared corrected editions of H. P. Lovecraft's work for Arkham House and annotated editions of the weird tales of Lovecraft, Algernon Blackwood, Lord Dunsany, M. R. James, Arthur Machen, and Clark Ashton Smith for Penguin Classics, as well as the anthology *American Supernatural Tales* (2007).

T. E. D. Klein is an American horror writer and editor.

Dean Kuhta is an artist and author. His current project is a new novel called *Silvarum,* an epic tale that follows three teenage siblings as they journey through a fantastic world of monsters and magic. More information can be found at www.deankuhta.com.

James Machin is a London-based scholar with an interest in early weird fiction, among other things. He is the co-editor of *Faunus,* the journal of the Friends of Arthur Machen.

Brian L. Mullen III is an artist, a musician, and curator for Ars Necronomica. Some of his work can be found at https://www.instagram.com/mulletofdeth.

Daniel Pietersen is a writer of weird fiction and horror philosophy. He has a blog of fragmentary work and other thoughts at https://constantuniversity.wordpress.com.

June Pulliam teaches courses on horror fiction at Louisiana State University. She is the author of *Monstrous Bodies: Feminine Power in Young Adult Horror Fiction,* as well as many articles on fantastic young adult fiction, Roald Dahl, and zombie studies.

Dr. Géza A. G. Reilly is a writer and critic with an interest in twentieth-century American genre literature. A Canadian expatriate, he now lives in the wilds of Florida with his wife, Andrea, and their cat, Mim.

Jim Rockhill has contributed to books devoted to E. T. A. Hoffmann, M. R. James, J. Sheridan Le Fanu, Bob Leman, Jane Rice, and Clark Ashton Smith as well as articles and reviews for various publications, including *Supernatural Literature of the World, Horror Literature through History, Lost Souls, Dead Reckonings,* and *The Green Book.*

Darrell Schweitzer is an American writer, editor, and critic in the field of speculative fiction. Much of his focus has been on dark fantasy and horror, although he does also work in science fiction and fantasy. His latest book is *The Threshold of Forever: Essays and Reviews.*

Donald Sidney-Fryer is the author of *Songs and Sonnets Atlantean* (Arkham House, 1971), *Emperor of Dreams: A Clark Ashton Smith Bibliography* (Donald M. Grant, 1978), *The Atlantis Fragments* (Hippocampus Press, 2009), and many other volumes. He has written many books and articles on California poets and recently published his autobiography, *Hobgoblin Apollo* (Hippocampus Press, 2016).

Alex Smith is the author of *Hive,* a weird horror novella published by Muzzleland Press. His horror-fantasy story "Snow River" appears in the anthology *Terror in 16-bits.* Alex was born in Washington, DC, and works in the DC/MD/VA area as a clinical psychologist.

Michelle Souliere works down in the bookmines at the Green Hand Bookshop in Portland, Maine, occasionally emerging from the vasty bookdeeps to scrawl charcoal, pencil, and ink on any surface she can find. She is also the author of the book *Strange Maine: True Tales from the Pine Tree State.*

Elena Tchougounova-Paulson has worked as head of the communications department and later as a research fellow and publisher at the Research Information Centre at the Russian State Archive of Literature and Art, Moscow. She is now an independent researcher, residing in Cambridge. Her subjects are Russian Literature, American Literature, Textual Studies, Theory of Literature, and History of Literature.

Bev Vincent is the author of several books, most recently *The Dark Tower Companion.* His work has been nominated for the Bram Stoker Award (twice), the Edgar Award, and the ITW Thriller Award, and he won the 2010 Al Blanchard Award. His reviews also appear at *Onyx Reviews* (onyxreviews.com). He is a contributing editor with *Cemetery Dance* and has published more than eighty short stories. His web presence is bevvincent.com.

www.ingramcontent.com/pod-product-compliance
Lightning Source LLC
Chambersburg PA
CBHW061747020426
42331CB00006B/1377